The Enquiry

A Play

Charlotte Hastings

A SAMUEL FRENCH ACTING EDITION

SAMUEL FRENCH

FOUNDED 1830

SAMUELFRENCH-LONDON.CO.UK
SAMUELFRENCH.COM

CHARACTERS

Kate Walmer	*a prisoner*
Probyn	*chief officer*
Collins	*prison officer*
Frances Treadgold	*deputy governor*
Marcy	*a prisoner*
Marian Oates	*governor's clerk*
Laura Fenn	*governor*
Janet Graham M.D.	*medical officer*
Gow	*a prisoner*
Rev. John Shillitoe (The Rev. John)	*chaplain*
Valentine	*a prisoner*
Tom Walmer	*Kate's husband*

The action passes in the Governor's office in a women's open prison in the Midlands

ACT I	Thursday morning
ACT II	
Scene 1	Friday afternoon
Scene 2	Half an hour later
ACT III	Five minutes later

The author expresses her thanks and appreciation to Dr Christine Saville and C. H. Shoemake, Esq., O.B.E., for help with details of prison procedure.

PRODUCTION NOTE

This play is set in a busy modern prison. The pace must never flag. Dialogue must not hold up action. The Governor must cope with the routine and the paperwork even in a crisis. Therefore all the movements have been carefully worked out in the script, with entrances and exits timed to keep a continuous flow. If the players and producers will follow these directions they will find that many difficulties are smoothed away and the play will develop a pattern of movement especially designed for manipulating a large cast—even on a small stage—without fear of getting in each other's way or holding up the vital action. It is recommended that the green walls be used for the setting. Otherwise the stage may be extremely colourless, since the prisoner's clothes are dull, the uniforms of the prison officers dark, and the remaining characters may not wear bright colours.

COSTUME

The four prisoners wear straight-cut belted dresses of grey denim with white collars and cuffs edged with navy blue. Skirts must be two inches below the knee. KATE wears a navy blue woollen cardigan in Act I only. MARCY wears a scarlet cardigan throughout which gives a much-needed note of colour. VALENTINE and GOW do not wear cardigans. MARCY and GOW who do special work, wear yellow armbands on the right arm. They all wear thick black stockings and plain black lace-up shoes. Any prisoners with long hair must have it either tied back or pinned up. No jewellery is allowed in prisons except a wedding ring—in this case KATE and MARCY. COLLINS wears prison officer's uniform and wears her peaked cap throughout the play. PROBYN can wear a plain dark suit and white blouse. (If there is a breast pocket in the suit, a whistle chain can be showing.) She should wear black nylons and smart—but low-heeled—shoes. The CHAPLAIN wears a black cassock with a leather belt in Act I. After that he wears the clerical collar and black vest which has two pockets in it, to be used for his watchchain. The GOVERNOR, DEPUTY GOVERNOR and the GOVERNOR'S CLERK may wear smart clothes but nothing flashy, no very short skirts and no undue display of jewellery. The bruise on KATE's face should be only slight and for the last act it is better to remove it altogether, since in the "flashback" scene the time is eighteen months earlier—and there is no opportunity to change make-up during this part of the play.

The costumes used in this play may be hired from Charles H Fox Ltd, 25 Shelton Street, London WC2H 9HX

THE ENQUIRY

ACT I

The Governor's office in a women's open prison in the Midlands

The prison is a modern building and the Governor's office, though plain, is cheerful. The walls are a pleasant shade of sage green, with white skirtings. Doors and window-frames are also white and the doors are polished mahogany without panels. Three tall windows are angled along one side, giving an impression of height with only sky and clouds visible. The upstage window opens outwards. There is a door to the corridor in the back wall, which opens inwards, and the sign "Governor's Office" can be seen on reverse. The wall seen through the door gives the prison atmosphere outside the pleasant office: it is painted cream above and lighter green below: there are three signs one below the other: "Deputy Governor" and "Chief Officer" pointing off one way, "Medical Officer" pointing off the other. Another door leads off a side wall

Immediately the CURTAIN *rises, someone screams loudly off, and chaos breaks out—shouting, banging, running feet*

    Kate Walmer rushes in from the corridor, with Chief Officer Probyn behind her

Kate leaps on to the window-seat up stage, flings open the window and turns. At this moment a whistle blows loudly off, and there is a dead silence, into which she shouts her first line

Kate Don't touch me or I'll jump . . . !

Kate is twenty-seven and would be attractive if not distraught. She wears prison uniform of grey denim dress with a white collar and cuffs, black shoes and stockings and a navy cardigan. Probyn is in her early forties, pleasant and capable. She does not wear uniform, but a plain well-cut navy suit, plain crisp white blouse, black stockings and shoes. She stands holding the door open

Probyn Walmer, get down and don't be a fool!
Kate If you touch me, I'll jump.

    Officer Collins runs in from the corridor panting. She is fortyish, strongly built. She wears prison officers' uniform and peaked cap

Collins Miss Treadgold's coming up . . . (*She stops, seeing Kate*)

Probyn (*not taking her eyes off Kate*) Go down and tell them to get a safety net. Come back and wait outside—hurry!
Collins Yes, Chief.

Collins runs out

Probyn (*moving briskly to the window-seat*) Now, Walmer, you've not given any trouble before. Why start now?
Kate Keep away! (*She swings the window wider and nearly overbalances. She clutches the curtain*)
Probyn Stand still—don't look down! Do you hear me? Don't look down.

Kate slowly turns her head

That's better. Keep your eyes on me. Now, steady—(*she makes a cautious move forward, holding out her hand*) take my hand . . .
Kate No!

Frances Treadgold, the Deputy Governor, enters from the corridor. She is in her late thirties and attractive. She carries a clipboard of papers

Frances (*matter-of-factly*) Well, Kate, if you want to break your neck, that's your choice. You might remember—quite apart from the trouble you'll cause us—your husband will have to live with it afterwards—

Kate goes rigid against the curtains

—and the children.

There is a pause. Then Kate turns and hides her face in the curtains. She sobs harshly once. Frances closes the door and goes to the desk

She won't do it now. Leave us alone.
Probyn It's a risk.
Frances I'll take the responsibility. (*She looks at her papers*)

There is a knock on the main door and Marcy hurries in. She is seventy, small and spry. She wears prison uniform, with a red cardigan which has a yellow armband on the right sleeve. She carries a large florist's bouquet in cellophane

Marcy Please, ma'am—(*seeing Kate*)—ow . . .
Probyn (*quickly*) Not now, Marcy.
Marcy But these is for the Governor . . .
Frances Put them on the table, would you, Chief.

Probyn takes the flowers from Marcy and goes to the alcove table. Marcy runs to the door

Frances Oh, Marcy, fetch some coffee. Hot and very strong. Get Gow to make it.

Marcy Gow make coffee? D'you want it mucked up with an egg whisk **and** parsley floating on top . . .
Probyn Marcy.
Marcy Yes, Chief?
Probyn Move!
Marcy (*hurriedly*) Yes, Chief.

Marcy gives one last look at Kate then scuttles out. Probyn follows, closing the door behind her

Frances flicks the intercom

Frances Miss Oates? Will you bring up the correspondence? We're a little disorganized here, but don't let it worry you. Thanks. (*She takes a bunch of keys from the desk drawer and goes to the cabinet, talking all the time*) Come down when you're ready, Kate. I shan't ask you again. (*She unlocks the drawer and finds a file*) Whatever is wrong, it can't be worth killing yourself, or getting maimed—which might be worse. I suggest we sit down and talk things out. (*She relocks the cabinet and returns to the desk with the file. She puts the keys in the desk drawer*) We're here to help you. Just remember that.

There is knock at the main door

Come. (*She sits at the desk*)

Marian Oates, the clerk, enters, carrying a basket of papers. She is young and efficient

Come in, Marian, the Governor will be back from London any moment. Are we fairly clear?

Marian puts the basket on the desk. She glances at Kate and away again

(*Quietly*) Take no notice. (*Briskly*) So what have we got?
Marian These are for the Governor's signature. (*She puts a folder of letters on the desk*)
Frances Right.
Marian A couple of orders, if you would just initial them. (*She takes two sheets from the basket and gives them to Frances*)
Frances (*reading them briefly, initialling them, and handing them back*) Next.
Marian I could cope with this, but I thought you'd better see it first. (*She gives Frances an open letter from the basket*)
Frances Oh, no, not the Professor again?
Marian I'm afraid so. I suppose he means well, but . . .
Frances I'm sure he does. I'm equally sure our inmates wouldn't particularly appreciate a monthly illustrated lecture on the significance of the male element in early Greek sculpture.
Marian (*smiling*) They might appreciate the slides. (*She hands over a card*)

Frances Yes, indeed—a *very* well developed gentleman. Good heavens, within ten minutes we'd be sedating the entire audience. (*She returns the card*) The usual. The Governor regrets—but thank you most sincerely—make it flowery. Then file it and hope that's the last of him.

Kate suddenly slides to her knees on the sill, her face still hidden in the curtains. Frances and Marian glance over, then at each other. Frances nods

Anyone on report?
Marian One. Gow. She's specially asked to see the Governor.
Frances That's her privilege. Has Mrs Fenn got a memo?
Marian In the file.
Frances Anything else?
Marian Only the Governor's personal letters. (*She puts a pile of unopened letters on the desk*)

There is a knock on the main door

Frances Come in. Thank you, Marian.

Marian goes to the door

Marcy enters and stands aside. She carries a tray of coffee

Marcy Morning, miss.
Marian Good morning, Marcy.

Marian goes out, shutting the door

Marcy goes to the desk and sees Kate

Marcy Blimey—she still up there . . .
Frances (*writing*) That will do, Marcy. Just put the tray here.

Marcy puts the tray on the desk, goes to the door and turns

Marcy Please, miss . . .
Frances (*continuing to work*) What is it?
Marcy You wouldn't have a fag, miss dear, would you?
Frances How many have you got already?
Marcy Not a whiff, I swear it. I'll turn out my pockets if you like.
Frances Last time, I remember, you had them in your pants.
Marcy Not any more, miss dear. When they get warm it spoils the flavour.
Frances Oh, really. Here. (*She pushes over the cigarette box*)

Marcy pounces on it

(*Warningly*) One only!
Marcy Thank you, miss dear. You're all right, you are. (*She runs to the door and turns with the cigarette in her hand*) Miss dear, you wouldn't have a king-size, would you? You can cut them in half and make two . . .
Frances No, I would not. Take that and get out before I take it back.

Marcy (*hastily*) Yes, miss dear. And bless and thank you for a good, kind . . .
Frances Move!
Marcy Yes, miss.

Marcy glances at Kate, rolls up her eyes and scuttles out

Frances (*blotting her writing*) Come and have some coffee, Kate. You needn't talk unless you want to.

After a second, Kate slowly gets off the sill and moves to the middle of the room, keeping a hand to the right side of her face

That's better. (*She gets up and moves to Kate, between her and the window*) Shall we sit down? It's very good coffee. Gow's special. (*She puts an arm round Kate*)
Kate (*jerking violently away*) No . . . ! (*She runs for the window*)

Frances catches her firmly, pulling one arm behind her back

(*Screaming*) Let me go! (*She wrenches herself free, trips and falls, supporting herself with her hands*)

Laura Fenn enters by the main door, followed by Probyn carrying a suitcase. Laura is nearly sixty, tall and with a considerable air of authority. She is handsome in a dark, strong-featured way; her face is severe but softened by the calm eyes and sensitive mouth. She is well dressed in a dark travelling suit, hatless, a short fur jacket over her shoulders, and she carries a handbag and gloves

Laura Good morning, Frances. Would you close the window, please.

Frances closes the window. Laura goes to the desk to put down her bag and gloves

I should have been here earlier—(*casually, in passing*)—get up, Kate—but the train was delayed at Langton, so of course I missed the connection. (*She gives Probyn her coat*) Thank you, Chief. Please stay within call a little longer.
Probyn Yes, madam.

Probyn goes out, closing the door

Laura (*going and sitting at the desk*) Kate, I do not speak merely for the pleasure of hearing myself do so. I told you to get up.

Kate does not move. Frances steps towards her, but Laura checks her

Get up, Kate.

Kate slowly gets up

Stand over here. In front of the desk.

Kate stands resting one hand on the upright chair, her back to the audience, head bent, shoulders drooping

Thank you. (*She takes her spectacles from her bag and puts them on. To Frances*) Is there anything important in the correspondence?

Frances No. Miss Oates has dealt with most of it. The letters are in the file.

Laura. Good. (*She sorts quickly through the private letters without opening them, then sits back*) Now, Kate. Why . . . ?

Kate does not answer

Answer me, Kate. (*With sudden authority*) And stand upright when I speak to you.

Kate jerks upright away from the chair, but keeps her head bent

That's better. I'll ask you again. Why?

Kate (*very low*) I—wanted to die.

Laura That is often easy, but seldom expedient. And if you answer one question by posing another, we shall get nowhere. So. Why did you want to die?

Kate It doesn't matter.

Laura You have only eight weeks before your release. Therefore it matters very considerably. Have you had bad news from home?

Kate shakes her head

Have you been feeling ill?

Kate shakes her head

You know that in an emergency you may ask to see me at any time. Did you do that?

Kate No, madam.

Laura Or to see Miss Treadgold?

Kate (*woodenly*) No, madam.

Laura (*to Frances*) Please ask Miss Probyn to come in. You may sit down, Kate.

Kate sits in front of the desk, still with her back to the audience and her head bent. Frances goes to the door and opens it to bring in Probyn

Probyn enters and stands in front of the door

Thank you, Chief, before this incident how recently had you seen Walmer?

Probyn This morning, ma'am. At breakfast.

Laura Did she appear in any way upset?

Probyn No, ma'am. I spoke to her about some work. She was perfectly normal.

Laura I see. (*She refers to the clipboard*) After breakfast you should have cleaned your room and reported to your working party for gardening duty. What happened then?

Kate does not answer

(*Abruptly*) Take your hand from your face.

Kate does not move. Laura goes to her, pulls her hand away and tilts up her face

Where did you get that bruise?

Kate remains silent

Now come along, Kate.
Kate I must have knocked it on the window catch.
Laura Miss Treadgold, I think you're about the same height.

Frances gets on the sill, opens the window and leans against it. It is obvious she is nowhere near the catch

So that won't do, Kate, will it?

Kate drops her head. Her hair, which is fairly long and has already come loose, falls across her face. Laura, who has been watching her intently, takes an elastic band from the desk tray and holds it out

Laura Put your hair off your face.

Kate slowly does so. As she puts an arm behind her head, she winces slightly

Have you hurt your arm?
Kate (*too quickly*) No, madam. (*She pauses, still with her hand behind her head, looking straight at Laura*)
Laura (*gently but firmly*) All right, Kate. Take off your cardigan.

Kate swings round on the chair to face Laura, For the first time her face is fully seen

Kate Please, madam . . .
Laura Take off your cardigan and unfasten your dress.
Kate Don't make me . . .
Laura It would be more dignified for you if I did not have to ask the Chief Officer.

Probyn takes a step forward. Kate immediately turns away and unfastens her cardigan. She takes it off and puts it on the desk. She unzips her dress to the waist and sits still, hands in her lap, head bent. Laura moves behind her and gently draws her dress down, exposing her shoulders. Frances and Probyn move down to see. They all look at one another. Laura picks up the telephone. Probyn gently drapes the cardigan over Kate's shoulders

(*On the telephone*) This is the Governor. Put me through to the hospital, please . . . Hullo—is Dr Graham there this morning? . . . Good. This is an emergency. Please ask her to come to my office at once. She had better bring a sedative . . . Yes, immediately . . . Thank you. (*She sits at her desk and opens the letter file*) We can't hold things up. Would you mind giving me a hand? I don't want Miss Oates here just now.

Frances Of course.

Laura starts signing letters. Frances blots each one and puts it in the envelope. Laura hands her one letter

Laura You might glance at that. I think you'll want to check that reference from your file.

A bell clangs loudly off. Under the windows hurrying feet are heard. A voice calls, "Into your lines. Smartly there." The whistle blows again and feet are heard marching away. Laura goes to the window and looks down as the sounds die out

(*Half to herself*) The answer's down there somewhere . . .

There is a knock at the main door

Come in. (*She sits at the desk*)

Dr Graham enters. She is a brisk, plump little Scotswoman of about fifty-five—very down to earth. She wears a white coat

Dr Graham Good morning, Governor.

Laura Thank you for coming so promptly, Doctor. Something for you to look at.

Probyn removes Kate's cardigan and stands back. Dr Graham moves behind Kate

Dr Graham M'm. Been in the wars, haven't we? All right, dear—just relax a moment. Could we have a glass of water, please?

Probyn goes to the main door

Collins is outside

Probyn speaks to Collins, then closes the door

We'll just have a look, shall we? (*She puts on her spectacles and stands looking at Kate's back. Then she draws the dress up*)

Kate flinches

No, I won't touch you. That's it. Now let's see your face. (*She turns Kate's chair so that she is back to the audience*) Right—turn to the light. You're lucky, my girl, it won't be a black eye. Now, can you tilt your head back—keep quite still. (*She takes a small torch from her pocket and examines Kate's eyes, then feels her pulse*)

There is a knock on the main door. Probyn opens it

Collins is outside with a carafe of water and a tumbler

Probyn takes them and shuts the door

Dr Graham Any headache?

Kate shakes her head

Good. Ah, thank you, Chief. Now, where did I put . . . (*She searches in her pockets and produces a bottle of tablets*) Here we are. Dress her up and give her a couple of these. Keep her warm. (*She gives Probyn the bottle and jerks her head to Laura and Frances to follow her out of hearing*)

Probyn helps Kate to dress and gives her the tablets and water

Nasty little business. Do we know who did it?
Laura Not yet.
Dr Graham Have to find out, eh? And she won't tell you, naturally.
Laura How serious is it?
Dr Graham Oh, not bad. No head injury. She'll be a bit stiff for a day or two. Probably going to be more serious for you than for her.
Laura I'm afraid so.
Dr Graham Well, that's your department. I think we'll have her in hospital for twenty-four hours. Tuck her up and keep her warm. Settle her down, you know.
Laura May I talk to her first? Before she has time to—to harden up? What about shock?
Dr Graham Certain amount, of course. How long would you want?
Laura A quarter of an hour?
Dr Graham Shouldn't do any harm. Provided you go easy. Give her a hot drink. Is that coffee there?
Frances It will be cold by now—shall I order some more?
Laura Would you, please?
Frances Do you particularly want me for the moment? I do have one or two urgent things . . .
Laura No, no—carry on. I do want a chat with you later. Perhaps I could ring down.
Frances Yes, of course. I'll send someone back with this.

Frances exits with the coffee-pot

Dr Graham (*briskly*) Well, that's that. You'll want me later, I've no doubt.
Laura It looks like it.
Dr Graham Yes. Very unpleasant. Do all I can, of course. Still, it's all in a day's work. I'll have a word with Matron. (*She picks up the pills and smiles at Kate*) Cheer up, dear. You'll live.

Dr Graham exits

Laura Thank you, Chief. I'll send for Miss Collins in about a quarter of an hour. Ask her to bring a top coat. She's to go over to the hospital.
Probyn Yes, madam.

Probyn exits

Laura Are you fairly comfortable now?

Kate Yes, thank you, madam.

Laura sits at her desk

(*Abruptly*) Madam . . .

Laura Yes, Kate?

Kate Do I have to go into hospital?

Laura Dr Graham thinks it would be best. (*Pausing*) It would be better still if you would tell me about it.

Kate I can't, madam.

Laura Kate, you are not a typical prisoner. (*She opens the file Frances took from the cabinet*) You are intelligent, well educated—university—I see you took a degree in history.

Kate (*harshly*) It hasn't counted for much, has it?

Laura It will in the future. And you do have a future. You must hold on to that. So many people here have absolutely nothing, in spite of what we do.

Kate Yes.

Laura I am going to speak to you plainly. And I should appreciate your speaking freely to me in return. Will you do that?

Kate I cannot tell you what you want to know.

Laura What I need to know. This is a very serious matter and cannot be overlooked.

Kate You mean there will have to be some sort of enquiry?

Laura Yes. And if you answer now, it will save a great deal of trouble and even more time.

Kate Madam—may I say something? Could you forget the whole matter, and accept it as part of my punishment?

Laura No, Kate. I could not and you know that. It is completely illogical . . .

Kate What has logic got to do with it? It is part of my punishment. Even a layman knows prisoners loathe another prisoner who has—

Laura Kate!

Kate —who has killed her own child.

Laura (*after a pause; quietly*) I did not want to mention that.

Kate It is the main issue. You knew that all along. You have asked me "who"—not "why".

Laura I am asking you that now.

Kate You want me to name someone, and that person will be punished—and humiliated—and it will be my fault. Always my fault. (*She jumps up and leans on the desk. Desperately*) Please—don't add one misery to another. For God's sake—isn't there enough in this place already?

Laura Sit down, Kate.

Kate I do beg of you . . .

There is a knock at the door

Laura Just a moment. (*Quietly*) Sit down, Kate.

Kate slowly sits. Laura moves behind her and puts a hand on her shoulder

Are you quiet now?

Kate nods

Laura opens the door

Collins is outside with a coffee-pot. Laura takes it with a quick word of thanks, and shuts the door

Kate I'm sorry—I . . .

Laura (*pouring coffee*) Drink this. (*She gives Kate a cup, pours one for herself, and stands looking out of the window and drinking. After a moment*) Why history?

Kate What?

Laura Your degree. Why did you read history?

Kate I have always been deeply interested in people. (*Wryly*) And history is safe.

Laura Safe?

Kate All the emotions are past.

Laura As our own will be eventually. It is a comforting thought.

Kate No emotions, good or bad, are comforting. We should have been born without them.

Laura The Lord in His infinite wisdom created us as we are. We can only trust Him that He knew what He was doing.

Kate You believe in God, then?

Laura I find it difficult to believe we all evolved from some amorphous blob of jelly. That may be old-fashioned—or simply arrogant. I only know that without my particular form of faith I could not have done this work.

Kate You have a tremendous quality of compassion. Are you never torn between what you want to do and what you know you must?

Laura Inevitably.

Kate How do you decide?

Laura One falls back on the rules.

Kate (*bitterly*) The great and glorious letter of the law.

Laura Yes.

Kate I should not be talking to you like this.

Laura For the moment we are not being official.

Kate I would like to say—officially—I do regret that I lost control and caused you this extra complication.

Laura Tell me something I don't understand. If you could accept this beating as part of your punishment, why should it make you want to kill yourself? (*She finishes her coffee and puts it on the desk*)

Kate (*slowly*) It was—the vicious hatred involved. It is terrible to realize one has done something which arouses such hatred in others.

Laura It is only fair to remember these—others—do not know the full situation.

Kate It is enough for them to know what I did.

Laura The circumstances were not normal. (*Gently*) Neither was the child.

Kate Does that give me absolution?

Laura It gave you a sympathetic hearing and a light sentence.

Kate The sentence is not in the law. It is in the mind.

Laura For someone like you—yes. But you must not carry it with you for ever. You'll be free soon. And we've agreed you have a great deal to live for.

Kate No-one has the right to take a life—(*breaking*)—however hopeless —and—distorted . . . (*She covers her face with her hands*)

Laura I'm not here to judge you, Kate. You were driven out of your mind by an intolerable and pitiful burden. One day, please God, a more sane and enlightened society may make such an action as yours unnecessary. (*She goes to the telephone*) The Governor speaking. Please ask Miss Collins to come to my office . . . Thank you. (*She replaces the receiver and turns to Kate*) Try and rest now, Kate. Then I shall probably change your work. If you want to see me at any time, just tell Matron.

Kate You are not asking me any more . . .

Laura No. I think your reasoning is wrong, but I cannot force you.

Kate You'll find out, of course.

Laura Yes, I think we shall.

Kate Be merciful. They are really not to blame.

Laura You must leave that to me.

There is a knock on the main door

Come in.

Collins enters carrying a coat over her arm

Ah, Miss Collins, will you take Walmer over to the hospital.

Collins Yes, ma'am.

Laura Help her on with her coat. (*She returns to signing letters*)

Miss Collins helps Kate with the coat, then opens the door

Kate (*formally*) Good morning, madam. And thank you.

Laura Good-bye, Kate. (*She turns to the intercom*)

Kate exits, followed by Miss Collins, who closes the door

(*On the intercom*) Miss Oates? Will you come up in about five minutes. Bring your notebook. Thank you. (*She continues working*)

There is another knock

(*With a sigh*) Come in.

Marcy puts her head round the door

Marcy 'Morning, Governor dear. Is it all right to collect the coffee-cups?

Laura Yes. Take them. (*She goes on working*)

Marcy moves to the desk and takes a yellow duster from her pocket with a flourish

Marcy All this hullaballoo and I've not done the dusting for you today. Shall we 'ave a quick flip then. (*She picks up the cigarette box, holding it in the duster and rubbing vigorously*)

Laura (*not looking up*) Not now. Take the tray and go.

Marcy Yes, ma'am. Perhaps the Chief'll let me finish you off this afternoon. Can't have you growing cobwebs, can we?

Laura Out, Marcy.

Marcy Yes, Governor dear. (*She tucks the duster back in her belt and replaces the box, then picks up the tray and goes to the door*)

Laura Marcy.

Marcy Yes, ma'am?

Still not looking up, Laura taps the cigarette box

Laura Put them back, Marcy.

Marcy Oh, really, ma'am.

Laura At once.

Marcy returns to the desk puts down the tray, takes the duster from her belt and picks four cigarettes from the folds. She puts them in the box

Marcy Some people've got eyes and ears in places they've no right to 'ave 'em.

Laura (*looking up*) That will do. And don't insult me by trying that old trick again.

Marcy I got to keep me 'and in, ma'am.

Laura Don't be impertinent.

Marcy Beg pardon, ma'am. (*She takes the tray and moves to the door*)

Laura (*looking in the box*) Marcy, I am ashamed of you.

Marcy I don't understand, ma'am.

Laura There were nine in the box. There are only eight here. Put that last one back.

Marcy But, ma'am, Miss Treadgold . . .

Laura Miss Treadgold does not smoke.

Marcy No more she does. But she gave me one this morning.

Laura Is that the truth?

Marcy (*running to the desk and putting down the tray*) Governor dear, would I lie to you?

Laura Without scruple.

Marcy I swear it, ma'am. I'd run right out, see, and when I brought the coffee, I asked her—for Gawd's sake, miss, I says, give us a fag, and she give me one. Not being flinty-hearted . . .

Laura Marcy.

Marcy stops and gulps

Are you sure this is correct?

Marcy On my oath, madam. (*She raises her right hand and gabbles*) I-swear-by-Almighty-God-that-the-evidence-I-shall-give . . .

Laura That's enough! Now, listen to me.

Laura's tone is not harsh, but Marcy automatically comes to attention

Through your own fault, you have wasted the greater part of your life in prison. I personally have no wish to make it harder for you. Do you understand that?

Marcy (*subdued*) Yes, ma'am.

Laura Because of your age, you are treated very leniently. But there cannot be one set of rules for you and another for everyone else. If you persist in this petty pilfering, I shall have no alternative but to punish you. Severely. Is that quite clear?

Marcy Yes, ma'am.

Laura So remember. Now, go.

Marcy takes the tray to the door

Marian enters

Marian Hallo, Marcy.

Marcy tucks her head down and scuttles out. Marian shuts the door

Cigarettes again?

Laura Yes.

Marian Poor old thing.

Laura It is not funny. She thinks she can clown her way out of everything. I will not have her encouraged.

Marian I beg your pardon.

Laura (*ruefully*) Oh dear, I didn't mean to snap at you. This is a difficult day and there's more to come. Please sit down. We have a lot to get through.

Marian sits and opens her notebook on her knee

Laura (*taking off her spectacles and passing a hand across her eyes*) I expect you know what has happened.

Marian I should think everyone does by now.

Laura Yes, indeed—this infernal grapevine. (*She replaces her spectacles*) Well, now, I'm arranging an informal discussion. Tomorrow at two-thirty. In this office. Send memos—I'll sign them—to Miss Treadgold, the Chief Officer, Dr Graham and the Chaplain. Got that?

Marian Yes, ma'am.

Laura And send a separate note to the chaplain. Ask him to have lunch with me first. One o'clock. In my sitting-room, I think.

Marian Shall I tell cook?

Laura Please ask her for something light—oh, and remember he's a strict vegetarian. (*She breaks off*)

A peculiar squeaking noise is heard outside

What on earth is that?

Marian Valentine taking the clean laundry round.

Laura But why that hideous noise?

Marian It's her little cart—it wants new tyres. We've indented for them weeks ago. (*She looks out of the window*) Yes, she's just crossing the courtyard.

Laura Then for heaven's sake get another request in. Ask one of the clerks to attend to it. It's quite nerve-racking.

Marian (*returning to her seat and making a note*) I'll do it right away.

Laura Thank you. Now, where were we . . .

Marian Lettuce for the padre.

Laura Oh yes. About the actual meeting—I'll leave you to arrange chairs and so on. I shall want Walmer's record. And when you write to Miss Probyn ask her for a list of everyone on the garden working party. I'll want you, too. To take notes.

Marian Yes, ma'am.

Laura You can take these—(*she puts the signed letters in the basket*)—and these. (*She adds the letters already in envelopes*) You'd better see what Miss Treadgold has for you. If it's rather much, one of the other typists can do it. I'll go through this private mail and then you can come back this afternoon and we'll try and finish.

Marian gets up and collects the basket

I'm afraid you're rather overloaded.

Marian We'll cope.

Laura Tell the switchboard to take all calls for me tomorrow afternoon. Nothing to be put through unless it's absolutely urgent.

Marian makes a note

I think that's all—no, one other thing. Better get a supply of cigarettes for Dr Graham. You know her brand.

Marian (*smiling*) I should do, by now.

Laura Yes, indeed. She certainly gives us every opportunity. (*She takes her keys from the desk drawer, crosses and unlocks the filing cabinet*)

Marian By the way, did you see your flowers?

Laura Flowers?

Marian They came this morning. I told Marcy to bring them up.

Laura Now who would be sending me flowers? (*She kneels to the bottom drawer*) Is there a card?

Marian (*bringing the flowers to the desk*) It's a letter.

Laura (*absently, intent on a file*) Open it, will you?

Marian (*opening the letter*) Why, madam, it's from Mrs Truscott!

Laura Mrs Trus . . . Read it out. I haven't got my glasses.

Marian (*reading*) "Dear Madam, I been to the Lady and she has read the letter you wrote first. She has given me the job to clean the house and answer the phone no cooking there is a cook here and she is a good sort and won't hold nothing against me. I have a nice room to myself and good time off. It is wonderful like heaven and I hope after all you've done for me to keep right and stay"—she's crossed something out here

—oh, yes—"to keep right and stay same yours respectfly Mrs Ann Truscott."

Laura Well, I . . .

Marian There's a P.S. "Dear Madam, I send these flowers as I know you like them they are for your room and God bless you for all you've done."

Laura (*going to the desk and taking the letter*) Who would have thought her capable?

Marian It's rather moving, isn't it?

Laura They must have cost her more than a week's salary.

Marian You really did try for her, ma'am.

Laura One tries so often. (*She touches the flowers, then puts the letter on the desk and replaces the keys in the drawer*) We must answer this.

Marian Will you dictate it now?

Laura No. It must be a personal letter and I need to think about it. I'll call you on the intercom later. We must put these in water.

Marian Would you like me to do it?

Laura Do you know, I think we'll let Gow do it. Cooking and arranging flowers are a passion with her. It will give her enormous pleasure and she does it beautifully.

Marian Madam . . .

Laura Yes?

Marian I'm afraid she's on report.

Laura Oh, no.

Marian gives her a file from the desk

Again. Yes, I see. Why does she—it's all so pointless and trivial. (*She looks at her watch*) Where can I fit this in—I think I had better do it now. (*On the phone*) Please ask the Chief Officer to bring Gow to my office . . . Thank you. (*To Marian*) We really could have done without this. Still, as Dr Graham would say, it's all in a day's work.

The telephone rings

And here we go again. Answer it, will you? (*She busies herself at the desk*)

Marian (*on the phone*) Governor's office . . . Would you hold on, please. (*To Laura*) The Rev. John.

Laura (*on the phone*) Hullo, Padre . . . Yes. Yes . . . It would have to be very brief. Could you come up now? . . . Good (*She replaces the phone*) Now—we must get organized. Let me think—look, see the Chief, would you? Ask her to keep back Gow for about ten minutes. Then get along to Miss Treadgold. Thank you very much.

Marian collects the basket and exits, shutting the door

Laura reads the letter again. The squeaking cart is heard. She exclaims impatiently, gets up and goes to the window, opening it and leaning out, looking down. There is a knock on the main door

(*Shutting the window*) Come in.

The Rev. John enters. He is about fifty, with grey hair, alert, humorous and a determined optimist. He wears his long cassock

Rev. John Good morning, Governor.
Laura Hullo, Padre.
Rev. John I won't keep you a moment. I was over at Wellesley all morning and I've only just heard . . .
Laura About Kate? Who from?
Rev. John The Chief Officer.
Laura Then you have the correct information.
Rev. John I just wanted to know if there's anything I can do. Would you like me to see Kate? Do you think she might confide in me?
Laura I very much doubt it, but please do see her. Have a word with Dr Graham first.
Rev. John Naturally. Is there any other way—any way at all—I can be of help?
Laura Could you be free tomorrow, from midday on? You will have a note from Miss Oates, so I won't go into details.
Rev. John Certainly, only too glad. This is a wretched business, Laura. I'm sorry.
Laura We've met it before.
Rev. John Unfortunately. But one is always grieved when it happens again, expecially in an open place like this. Don't drive yourself too hard, my dear. You look weary.
Laura An occupational disease we all share.
Rev. John I'm afraid so. But you will handle this. And you'll have my full support—in every way. Just let me know if I am needed. Any time.
Laura Thank you.
Rev. John I won't keep you any longer. God bless you.
Laura Before you go, you might like to read this. Something a little brighter, just for a change. (*She gives him the letter*) You won't mind if I go on . . .
Rev. John No, no, don't mind me.

Laura sits at her desk and writes

(*Reading the letter*) Well, this really is most gratifying. I'm delighted for you. And you deserve it.
Laura No more than anyone else concerned.
Rev. John I know better. We must follow this up—keep the contact.
Laura Yes, I'm going to write a personal letter.
Rev. John Would you like me to write as well?
Laura A very good idea. I feel the more encouragement she gets——
Rev. John —especially at the beginning. I'll just take a note of the address if I may. (*He takes out a small notebook and scribbles*) And now I really will leave you in peace. Don't forget. Any time.

Laura Padre, Kate still doesn't want to speak. I think we should respect her reasons.

Rev. John I understand. (*He opens the main door*)

Probyn is standing outside with Gow, and carries a report book. The Rev. John stands back for them

Rev. John Good morning, Chief. Good morning, Gow.

Probyn Good morning, sir. (*To Gow*) The Chaplain spoke to you.

Gow mutters something inaudible

The Rev. John glances at her, then at Laura, and exits

Gow is about thirty, tall, dark, almost foreign looking, and in a tense and smouldering temper. She wears the prison uniform and a yellow armband

Forward to the Governor's desk. Smartly. Back straight. Hands behind you. (*To Laura*) Gow, madam. On report.

Laura Read her the charges.

Probyn Disobedience, swearing. Fighting in the kitchen. (*She puts the book before Laura*)

Laura (*studying it*) Have you anything to say?

Gow (*sullenly*) Why should I? You got it all down there.

Laura Yes, it's all here. For the third time in six weeks. Insubordination, bad language—always the same. Just what is this feud between you and Mrs Beatty?

Gow She can't cook.

Laura She has been employed here in that capacity for seven years.

Gow She's not trained. I am.

Laura Indeed you are. That is why you are allowed to work in the kitchen. Work. Not criticize, and make trouble. And particularly not to throw saucepans. It is disgraceful behaviour.

Gow Permission to speak, ma'am.

Laura Yes?

Gow (*becoming more worked up*) It's downright bloody wicked . . .

Probyn Watch it now!

Gow Well, it is. Call herself a cook! Good food comes into this place. No-one can complain about that. And what does she do? Bloody ruins it—burns it, shrivels it, or else it's raw. Why, the only way she knows to cook cabbage is bloody drown it . . .

Laura That's enough. You will please speak to me without swearing. And don't forget I personally taste the food every day. No-one else complains.

Gow They either don't know different, or they haven't the bl . . . haven't the guts.

Laura Then it's a pity you haven't the guts to control yourself. You have been warned again and again . . .

Gow Wicked waste of the taxpayer's money. It makes me boil, sod it . . .

Laura That will do! If you use another swear word during this interview you will go straight to the punishment room. Right?

Gow (*woodenly*) Ma'am.

Laura I've been very patient with you. Because of your aptitude, you've been allowed to do work you like. You cannot expect to take over the entire kitchen, however much you think you are qualified. I've given you chance after chance to behave yourself, and I will not tolerate any more. Take off your armband.

Gow claps her hand tight over her armband

Chief . . .

Probyn moves. Gow whips off the band

Put it on the desk.

Gow throws it there

Thank you. (*She puts it in the desk drawer*) From now on you will work in the laundry.

Gow Laundry!

Laura Yes. You will now go away and try to behave yourself. When you think you are in a proper state of mind, you may ask to come and see me. You will then apologize and tell me you are ready to take back the band. And I may consider—I say consider, mind—letting you return to the kitchen. Thank you, Chief.

Probyn About turn. Smartly, and out.

Laura Just a moment. Before you start your punishment you may do something for me. Something you do extremely well. Take those flowers and put them in water.

Gow I . . .

Laura You may bring them back here and put them in the alcove. I shall not ask an officer to come with you. Then you will report to Miss Probyn.

Gow does not move

Probyn (*sharply*) You heard what the Governor said.

Gow still does not move. Probyn holds out the flowers

Gow (*suddenly*) No! (*She dashes the flowers to the floor*)

Probyn seizes her, pulling her hands behind her back

I bloody won't!

Gow screams and struggles with Probyn, kicking and trampling the flowers. They both shout together. Laura goes and opens the main door

Probyn ⎧ Now then, that's enough! Stop this at once, at once, do you hear—control yourself . . .

Gow ⎨ You can stuff your blasted flowers! Thinks she can soft-soap me—I won't—I won't . . .

Laura Take her to the punishment room.

Probyn gets Gow, still struggling and screaming, through the main door. Laura closes it behind them. Gow is still heard shouting

Gow (*off*) Let me alone! You bitch—let me alone . . .

Laura returns to her desk, glances at her wrist watch, then flicks the intercom

Laura Frances? . . . How are you placed? . . . If we had a talk now, we should both have a free afternoon . . . Straight away? . . . Yes, please do. (*She goes to the bookshelves, finds a newspaper and spreads it on the desk. She picks up the mangled bouquet, finds three undamaged blooms, fills the glass used by Kate from the carafe, and puts the flowers in it. She rolls the debris in the paper and goes to the inner door*)

Laura exits through the inner door

Frances enters through the main door; Laura returns, dusting off her hands

Frances What was all that shouting?

Laura Gow. (*She sits at her desk*)

Frances (*sitting opposite*) It's getting rather frequent.

Laura Too much so. I think we may have to consider having her transferred.

Frances Oh, but . . .

Laura (*smiling*) I know how you feel. Confession of failure.

Frances Or shift of responsibility.

Laura We have a responsibility to the others.

Frances But she's never attacked anyone directly.

Laura So far as we know.

Frances You don't think it was she who . . .

Laura No. She was on kitchen duty all morning. She had no access to Kate.

Frances That's a relief. Laura, she isn't psychopathic. It's basically sheer uncontrollable temper . . .

Laura Which is getting rapidly worse. She'll have to be watched. And with our minimum security we haven't the facilities.

Frances If she was more restricted, she might really go to pieces . . .

Laura You heard her just now. What do you call that?

Frances Temper. Can't we sort out what caused this latest outburst, and give her another chance?

Laura I know what caused it. And if you look at her record you'll see it's inherent. Remand home, approved school, Borstal—never out of trouble. She was only sent here because she'd kept steady for five years.

Frances Then wouldn't it be a pity to throw her back among sharks?

Laura We shall have to think. I've taken her off kitchen work. If she does stay here, she'll work in the laundry.

Frances She won't like that.

Laura No-one is here to like anything. Prison is a deterrent—not a holiday camp. If we do our job correctly, none of them should want to return.

Frances Isn't it enough to lose their personal freedom?

*Laura signs the report book and puts it on top of the cabinet, speaking as
she crosses*

Laura They have a great deal of freedom here. They have comfortable
conditions and certain privileges. And that reminds me. It's a small thing,
but I feel I should mention it.

Frances Yes?

Laura I don't think Marcy should be given extra cigarettes.

Frances (*laughing*) What made her tell you?

Laura I did. She pulled that duster trick again—right under my nose.

Frances Oh, no—not with you?

Laura Yes. And it has to stop.

Frances (*still amused*) She'll never alter. She's the classic recidivist—out
for the summer and back in the winter. Prison's her home. She'll probably die in one.

Laura And that is a confession of failure. For us.

Frances I think you're taking it a little bit too seriously. She's quite harm-
less—

Laura —and cheerful and disarming and often very funny. I know. And
she should not be allowed to get away with it. She is here for punishment.

Frances (*laughing*) Oh, for heaven's sake—one cigarette!

Laura She has her allowance. It's a game, Frances. When she can, she
steals. If she can't steal, she wheedles. When she scores a point, she
cheerfully chalks it up against us, and plans her next move. It has got
to stop.

Frances Very well. I won't do it again if that's what you wish. But she's a
likeable old thing, in spite of her sins. One can't help feeling sympathy.

Laura I always find it so difficult to avoid sympathy becoming senti-
mentality.

Frances How does one divide these?

Laura By disciplining ourselves as well as the prisoners. (*Sighing*) Yes,
it is difficult. Don't think I don't realize that.

Frances I wish I had your strength.

Laura That comes with experience. You have your own kind. We belong
to different generations and one can only do the job as one sees it
personally. When I look back at my own mistakes . . .

Frances (*breaking in*) You have taught me a great deal, and it has been
a privilege to work with you.

Laura Thank you. (*Goes back to desk and sits. Briskly*) Now—this latest
business . . .

Frances Kate has told you nothing?

Laura No, and I don't think she can be persuaded.

Frances Nor anyone else for that matter.

Laura Not very easily, I agree.

Frances It will have to be referred.

Laura Yes. But the Home Office will want the full facts. We must try and
elicit them with as little delay as possible.

Frances (*nodding*) An enquiry.
Laura Unofficial. Two-thirty tomorrow. Here. Myself, you, the Chief, Dr Graham and the Chaplain.
Frances A judicious combination of the temporal and the spiritual.
Laura (*smiling*) Poor Rev. John will be somewhat outnumbered. We must keep Dr Graham in check. We know what they're like in argument.
Frances They enjoy it—every time she calls him a Sassenach, he feels ten years younger. (*She becomes more serious*) Laura, it is possible we might never find out.
Laura We shall. Make no mistake about that. I'll get to the bottom of it if it's the last thing I do in the service.
Frances Right. (*She goes to the main door*)
Laura Don't go, Frances. (*Moving to the windows*) While you are here, there's something else.

Frances returns into the room. Laura looks out of the windows, speaking with her back turned

This is strictly off the record.
Frances (*suddenly tense*) Yes?
Laura After the consultative board yesterday I saw Hovenden. (*Slowly*) I shall be retiring from the service in the spring.
Frances Shall you—be sorry?
Laura (*turning*) Yes and no. It has been a life's work, especially since my husband died. But I'm getting tired. And it's right I should make way for someone younger.
Frances Still off the record—has anyone been . . .
Laura (*quietly*) I am sure you will be among those considered. (*She sits at her desk, pulling some papers towards her*)
Frances I see.
Laura That shouldn't surprise you.
Frances Naturally, I had hoped . . .
Laura I thought you'd like to know.
Frances Thank you. (*She goes to the door and turns*)

Laura is writing

Laura—I should like to feel you would be in favour of my appointment.
Laura (*quietly*) The decision will be made by the Home Office.
Frances You are likely to be asked for recommendations.
Laura Perhaps. (*She looks up*) Frances, does this mean so much to you?
Frances Yes, it does.
Laura You realize you would be young to undertake it?
Frances You did say strength comes with experience.
Laura Yes, I did.
Frances If you think . . .
Laura Even in confidence you must not ask me any more.
Frances (*quietly*) It was generous of you to tell me so much. (*She turns to go*)
Laura Frances—

Frances turns

—be patient. You have one most precious asset. Time.
Frances Time—for me—is now.

Frances exits

Laura sits back in her chair. She visibly braces herself, then picks up Mrs Truscott's letter, glances at it, puts it down on the desk. She clicks the intercom

Laura (*on the intercom*) Miss Oates . . . A letter, please. On my private notepaper. To Mrs Truscott—you will have the address. Dear Mrs Truscott . . . (*She thinks for a second*) Dear Mrs Truscott. I am much moved—correction—deeply moved—by your gift of flowers. They are —very beautiful—and I have them before me on my desk . . . (*Smiling a little ruefully, she picks up the glass with the three salvaged blooms*)

CURTAIN

ACT II

SCENE 1

The same. Friday afternoon

The room has been arranged for the enquiry

As the CURTAIN *rises, Laura enters from the inner door, followed by the Rev. John. He now wears a lounge suit, clerical collar and black silk vest with a watch-chain across it. Laura carries a table napkin, which she drops on the drinks table as she moves to the bookcase. They are both laughing*

Laura We'll see who's right. It should be here somewhere. Help yourself to a brandy. I know it's not against your Christian principles.

Rev. John No, indeed. Praise God for the grape—and the knowledge to use it!

Laura Casuistry! (*She finds a book and turns the pages*)

Rev. John In moderation, of course. Shall I pour you one?

Laura Please. Yes, here we are. What was your version?

Rev. John (*pouring two drinks*) "For in that older time, when truth . . ."

Laura Wrong. Elder time—not older.

Rev. John Disgraceful. (*He comes down with two glasses, looking over her shoulder*) And translated by one of my cloth, I see, which makes it even worse. How does it go on . . .

Laura (*reading*) "For in that elder time when truth and thought were still revered and cherished here on earth . . ." (*She suddenly closes the book*) When truth and thought were still revered and cherished—elder time, indeed.

Rev. John Come, do I detect a note of bitterness? Unless my memory misserves me again, there's something further on about—hope and a great joy.

Laura (*putting the book on the desk*) It would be nice to think so.

Rev. John (*cheerfully*) Why, then—let's drink to it.

He gives her a glass and they drink

And now, what is it you want to ask me?

Laura (*laughing*) Has it been so obvious?

Rev. John You didn't invite me to that excellent lunch solely to discuss Caius Valerius Catullus. Though it has indeed been a refreshment for the mind as well as the stomach. (*Indicating the book on the desk*) Might I—in the language of my small nephew—have a lend of this?

Laura Please do.

Rev. John Thank you. So now—officially—what is the difficulty—if any?

Laura You know, I expect, that I'm retiring. By the way, I didn't tell you. I've been offered a lecture tour in America.

Rev. John You'll do it excellently. Have you thought of staying there for good?

Laura I'm an anachronism. I still find England both gracious and agreeable.

Rev. John Nevertheless, I do not see you in a country cottage with roses, books and music. And perhaps a dog for company.

Laura (*laughing*) I have always been inclined towards a Border collie.

Rev. John You'll die of frustration within six months.

Laura Certainly not. There is plenty of social service. I intend to be on every committee within a ten-mile radius.

Rev. John Then, apart from those inevitable moments of loneliness which must close on all of us, what is the problem?

Laura Frances.

Rev. John Ah. So she's in the running.

Laura Yes.

Rev. John And you will be approached?

Laura I suppose that is the heart of the matter.

Rev. John What shall you say?

Laura She is a most capable administrator, with modern ideas—and the burning zeal of the reformer.

Rev. John I find that both kind and scrupulous.

Laura It is a delicate evasion of the real issue.

Rev. John Which is . . .

Laura I feel—she speaks from impulse, acts on emotion, and is probably ten years too young.

Rev. John Then you should say so.

Laura But who am I to be didactic? She lives and works within her own generation. The work as I know it—the methods and the conditions— are all changing.

Rev. John What will never change is the need. You and others like you, have done fine work when conditions were deplorable. Frances may well work out her own way of progress . . .

Laura (*abruptly*) If progress means pampering and indulgence, we may as well close down all prisons and have done with it.

Rev. John You don't really think that . . .

Laura I think we may go to extremes. Perhaps we have come too far too quickly.

Rev. John (*gently*) It is not so very far back to the treadmill and the whipping post.

Laura That is brutality. I am talking about discipline.

Rev. John Discipline . . .

Laura I know, Padre, I know. Nowadays that has become a dirty word. And without, what have we? Ever increasing crime, and our so-called permissive society. With its drugs, its legalized abortion, and all other dreary ramifications.

Rev. John Laura . . .

Laura Permissive? Submissive. Submissive to any influence which avoids clear thinking and responsibility.

Rev. John There are no short answers. (*Sadly*) Or if there are, the Church, unhappily, has not yet found them.

Laura The Church has the complete answer, but because it is not an easy one, it is no longer acceptable.

Rev. John (*smiling*) The truth is clearly laid down and many still follow it. This is—not yet—an entirely Godless world. Remember? "Hope and a great joy."

Laura You are an incurable optimist.

Rev. John That is essential. Otherwise we should all eat the bread of our own bitterness, and there would be no beginning and no end.

Laura We are discussing this and saying nothing new. It has all been said again and again—the same arguments, the same clichés. Where are we wrong, Padre? What can we do?

Rev. John Pray. And search for the reasons.

Laura Reasons? Or excuses? And if you are going to tell me—it is all a sickness—or a question of glands—then I warn you, I have no more tolerance.

Rev. John I am just going to remind you that—in spite of it all—there are still the Mrs Truscotts.

Laura (*slowly*) Yes. Yes, there are. I'm sorry, Padre. One must not forget the Mrs Truscotts.

There is a knock at the door

Excuse me. Come in.

Marcy enters

The telephone rings

(*Exasperated*) For goodness' sake—wait there, Marcy. (*On the phone*) Yes? . . . Now? (*She glances at her watch*) All right, Matron. I think I can just manage. Very well. (*She replaces the receiver*) What is it, Marcy?

Marcy Please, Governor dear, I've come for the dishes.

Laura In there, and don't be too long.

Marcy exits to the inner room

Padre, Kate has asked to see me. It may be important. Will you wait? I think *The Times* is around somewhere. (*She takes it from the alcove table*) Yes, here.

Rev. John Laura—(*he puts a hand on her arm*)—be objective about this. We can't save others from making our mistakes. Or how would they learn? And in any case, this appointment is not—to use my own jargon —within your gift.

Laura looks at him for a second, then smiles and gives him the newspaper

Laura Don't do the crossword. I'm saving it for a nightcap.

Laura exits by the main door, closing it behind her. The Rev. John exits to the inner room

Marcy enters from the inner room with a tray of dishes which she puts on the drinks table

She then glances behind her, then gleefully goes to the table and takes a cigarette from the box. She tucks it behind her ear and collects the glass from the Governor's desk. The squeaking noise is heard off and she glances up, listening. She takes the glass to the drinks table and pauses, listening again. She goes to the main door and opens it, looking off

Marcy Val? What is it? . . . No, I can't. I'm busy. No. Only the Rev. The Rev. (*Louder*) Holy Joe! (*She claps her hand to her mouth, looking towards the inner room, then off again*) What? . . . Oh, all right—only for a minute.

Marcy exits, closing the main door.

The Rev. John enters and puts the newspaper on the bookcase, then crosses to the window-seat, takes a book from his pocket, and sits and reads.

Marcy hurries in again. She has a note in her hand. The cigarette is now going full blast in the centre of her mouth. She sees the Rev. John and hurriedly puts it behind her back

Oh, excuse me, sir. Shan't be a moment.
Rev. John That's all right, Marcy. You just carry on. (*He returns to his book*)

Marcy stubs out the cigarette on her shoe and puts it in her pocket. She reads the note, pursing her lips and shaking her head. She puts it in her pocket, goes to the drinks table and picks up the used glasses. She glances over at the Rev. John, then tips the dregs into one glass and drinks

(*Glancing up*) I'm glad to see you're busy.

Marcy swallows hard, puts the glass on the tray, and turns, beaming

Marcy Bless you, sir. I know my way round here, you see.
Rev. John So you should by now. When are you going to leave us for good? You're in and out as regularly as the calendar.
Marcy Well, I got the authority of the Scriptures, 'aven't I?
Rev. John What?
Marcy In the Bible. Plain as its own print. The Lord bless thy goings-out and thy comings-in.
Rev. John *Marcy!*
Marcy (*casting up her eyes*) Blessed be the name of the Lord.
Rev. John If you must turn Holy Writ to your own purpose, what about "forswear thy foolish ways"?
Marcy What else am I trained for? And my 'ands 'as lost their touch these days—(*she holds them out*)—it's the arthritis, see?
Rev. John (*gently*) There are other jobs, you know.
Marcy Oh, the odd bit of cleaning. But there again, I'm clumsy. I drop things. It don't really matter here—with the tough china and the Govern-

ment well able to buy us more—but private service don't look kindly on breakages.

Rev. John I might be able to get you some office cleaning. You wouldn't handle crockery.

Marcy I've tried to do that—but then it gets me in the knees. Old age isn't a blessing, you know. (*Sadly*) And to think I used to be one of the best "dips" in the business.

Rev. John And unfortunately proud of it.

Marcy Why not? It's a skilled profession. And my husband was a real expert. He could remember the old days. He often told me about the sovereigns. Sovereigns, Padre. Just picking up a quid in one go—easy as pulling a daisy.

Rev. John I'm very glad it's no longer possible. (*He puts his book in his pocket and gets up*)

Marcy It was progress ruined us old 'uns. D'you know what really took the joy out of it? Two things——

Rev. John (*laughing*) I shouldn't allow you to tell me.

Marcy —the wrist watch and the zip fastener. 'Course, some of the youngsters still manage. D'you know, Padre, I've seen a zip what's been cut out as sweet and neat as a bit of high-class surgery. But not by my stiff old fingers.

Rev. John Which is just as well.

Marcy And wrist watches, no. The old chain was the thing—with a fat ticker at one end and a sovereign purse at the other. Beautiful. And I see you wear one yourself. Very unusual these days, sir, if I may say so.

Rev. John (*laughing*) Hands off, Marcy. That belonged to my grandfather.

Marcy Could I have a look at your watch, sir? Go on, be a sport. Haven't seen a real good watch for years.

Rev. John Oh, very well. (*He takes out the watch on the end of its chain, keeping it firmly in his hand*)

Marcy Lovely workmanship, Victorian. And look at those links—all chased. (*She takes out her yellow duster and polishes the watch*)

Rev. John Now, now, Marcy—I'm very attached to that in more ways than one.

Marcy Bless you, sir, that's all right. You know how I like my little joke. (*She tucks watch back in his pocket, pats it, and goes for the tray*)

Rev. John Yes, we all know your little jokes.

Marcy Everyone's very kind about it. This is a good place. I've got my armband, a good bed and a few fags.

Rev. John And a little drop of brandy on the quiet.

Marcy (*turning*) Padre, you didn't . . .

Rev. John I'm afraid so.

Marcy You won't tell the Governor, will you? Please. I'm in bad with her already. Had me up yesterday. Laid me out with flowers , , ,

Rev. John And well deserved, I've no doubt. You mustn't let the Governor down. She's been very good to you.

Marcy One of the best, she is. No. I wouldn't want to hurt her—(*wheedling*)—just so's she don't know . . .

Rev. John You're incorrigible. Be off with you.

Marcy Yes, sir. Thank you, sir. (*She turns to the tray, then back again*) Padre, can you tell me the time?

Rev. John The . . . ? Marcy! (*He pulls out the chain. There is no watch at the end of it*)

Marcy hoots with glee, takes the watch from her duster, and shows it to him. He snatches it

Marcy I couldn't resist it, sir. You standing there so good and unsuspecting as a cherub. (*Tapping the watch*) Actually, I think it's a bit fast.

Rev. John (*sternly*) Now you listen to me, Marcy . . .

Frances enters followed by Marian, who carries a notebook and pencil. They cross to desk

Frances Hullo, Padre, Marcy.

Marcy (*hurriedly*) Just going, miss. (*She dives for the tray*)

Rev. John holds the door open for Marcy. As she passes him she winks

Saved by the bell!

Rev. John I'll see you later, you wicked old sinner!

Marcy exits

Marcy (*off*) Hi, Doctor. It's all go, isn't it?

Marian sits at the small table above desk and sets out pads and pencils from the small to the long table. Frances looks at a file

Dr Graham enters, she is not wearing her white coat, and carries a large envelope. Marian goes to her table and talks aside to Frances

Dr Graham Ah, Rev. John. Am I late?

Rev. John No. The Governor's not here yet. Come and sit down.

He sits at lower end of table. Dr. Graham above him

Dr Graham Let's hope we can sort this little lot out quickly. (*Opening the cigarette box*) And I see the Governor's pandered to my vice. My own brand, too.

Rev. John I thought you'd given it up. (*He gives her a light*)

Dr Graham No, that was last week.

Probyn knocks and enters. She puts some papers down on the desk

Probyn The Governor asked for this list, Miss Treadgold.

Frances Thank you, Chief.

Probyn sits at top end of table

Dr. Graham (*blowing smoke and coughing violently*) Lord save us, my first this afternoon—always gets me. Bang my back, Padre, will you—ouch! You needn't be so enthusiastic. D'you want to annihilate me?

Rev. John The way of the transgressor is hard.

Dr Graham So are your hands. That's better.

Laura enters

They all stand up

Laura I'm sorry to keep you waiting. (*She goes to the desk*) Please sit down. This is quite informal. But it may take time, so we might as well be comfortable. (*She sits at the desk and puts on her spectacles*)

Everyone sits down (see positions on plan)

I should tell you that I have just seen Kate. At her request.

Frances Has she said anything . . .

Laura She wanted to stress her first request to me. To drop the whole matter and regard it as part of her punishment.

Rev. John Creditable.

Dr Graham Impossible.

Laura Both. This will be an internal discussion and any results will be referred. The infuriating thing is that by now probably everyone—except the staff—knows the culprit.

Dr Graham And you'll never get it out of them.

Rev. John Could that not—even subversely—be a point in their favour?

Dr Graham They know damn well an informer might get the same treatment.

Rev. John You don't believe in honour among thieves?

Dr Graham I don't believe in thieves.

Laura Whatever the reason for this, it must not happen again.

Dr Graham That's not very likely. Child killers don't—thank God—come in weekly batches.

Laura (*quietly*) No. It might help to go, briefly, over Kate's record. (*She opens a file*)

From now on Marian takes notes

She came here last year, on a twelve-month sentence. She has been a model worker and has full remission. She leaves in about eight weeks. The circumstances were tragic . . .

Rev. John Aren't they always?

Laura In this instance, exceptionally. As we all know, she is intelligent, educated, and of good background. So is her husband. They have two other children, boys of four and six. The third child—a girl—was hopelessly abnormal . . .

Dr Graham Any medical details there?

Laura A few. Chief . . . (*She takes a page from the file*)

Probyn takes the page to Dr Graham

Dr Graham Yes—I see. This is really dreadful. Why do we allow such things to live? If it had been an animal it would have been put head down in a bucket.

Frances (*involuntarily*) Oh, don't!

Dr Graham Why not? What is the sane choice? Slide in a merciful needle
—or let it grow?

Rev. John And pray for a miracle.

Dr Graham (*tartly*) When the Creator makes a mistake of this magnitude
—(*tapping the paper*)—he does not, in my experience, see fit to put it
right.

Rev. John Now, you really can't . . .

Laura Please. We mustn't start a discussion about euthanasia.

Dr Graham Sorry, Governor.

Frances And there are institutions.

Dr Graham Yes—where we come up against sentiment. The mothers cling.
I've seen it so often. Normal children affected. Marriages broken up.

Laura Which is nearly what happened here.

Frances (*looking at the file*) But look—she kept the child for over a year.
After so long, wouldn't she have been persuaded to part with it, rather
than take its life?

Dr Graham How did she do that, by the way?

Laura Put a pillow over its face.

Dr Graham Dear Lord, how could she?

Rev. John We mustn't judge. You've seen many people break under
pressure.

Dr Graham (*grimly*) I've seen the results.

Frances Well, we've a pretty wide field. And apparently no starters.

Dr Graham If there were, my money would be on Gow.

Laura Obviously, I'm afraid. But she was nowhere near at the time.

Dr Graham Nowhere near where? Do we know where the assault took
place?

Laura Kate was with the gardening party. I think it must have happened
outside. Chief, would you ask Miss Collins to come in?

*Probyn goes to the main door. Collins is outside. She comes in and remains
by the door as Probyn returns to her seat*

The squeaking noise is heard again

Laura Is that Valentine again? Really—hasn't anything been done about
that awful noise?

Marian I put through another memo yesterday, madam.

Laura Well, keep track of it, will you? (*To Collins*) Miss Collins, please
tell us exactly what happened yesterday morning, as far as you know it.

Collins I spoke to Walmer after breakfast, madam. She was quite normal
then.

Laura Yes?

Collins The working party consists of fifteen prisoners.

Probyn If I may interrupt, madam. I have put the names on your desk.

Marian pushes over the list

Laura Thank you, Chief. Miss Collins . . . ?

Collins The party went out and split up as usual. They work in three groups of five, each with its own leader. Miss Barnes and I keep an overall watch.

Dr Graham But you can see every individual all the time.

Collins Yes. Yesterday all three groups were working in the vegetable garden. At ten-thirty we called the usual break for a rest and a cigarette if they wanted one.

Laura Yes.

Collins Miss Barnes and I were talking. Suddenly we saw Walmer running towards the main building. We realized that something was wrong. We ran after her.

Laura Both of you?

Collins She was obviously distressed. We thought she might be ill. She ran in the main door and met the Chief Officer in the hall . . .

Laura Chief?

Probyn I caught hold of her. She broke away and started up to this landing. I told Miss Collins to find the Deputy Governor and send Miss Barnes back to the working party. I followed Walmer up here.

Laura Thank you. (*To Collins*) Now think back carefully. Was anyone running—or starting to run—after Walmer?

Collins We saw no-one, madam.

Laura Did you hear anything? Shouting? Screaming?

Collins Nothing. Of course, when Miss Barnes got back everyone was working quietly as though nothing had happened.

Laura Thank you. Does anyone want to ask Miss Collins anything else?

Dr Graham and the Rev. John confer for a moment. Probyn looks over at the wall map. Dr Graham taps her arm. She turns, shakes her head and looks back at the map

Dr Graham No questions, Governor.

Laura Thank you, Miss Collins. That's all for the moment.

Collins exits

Probyn suddenly goes up to the wall map

Both I and the Chief have questioned the members of the gardening party. Without success. If you feel there is anything to be gained by questioning them again now . . .

Dr Graham Speaking for myself, if you and the Chief have made no impression I think it would be a waste of time.

Rev. John I quite agree.

Dr Graham Chief?

Probyn, still studying the wall map, does not answer

Chief?

Probyn (*slowly*) Madam, this map . . .

Laura Yes?

Probyn (*indicating*) The vegetable garden is backed by the yew hedge. Here. And here is an opening.
Frances A gap—yes.
Probyn If you go through—the reception wing is almost directly opposite. The main room is hardly ever used in the daytime. And the outer door isn't locked.
Dr Graham You think it might have happened there?
Rev. John Surely anyone trying to slip through the gap would be seen?
Probyn Look—the small toolshed is just by the opening. People are in and out and around that all the time.
Dr Graham It was more than one person.
Laura Why do you say that?
Dr Graham Someone held her. Bruises on both upper arms. (*She takes some cards from the envelope*) I didn't think you'd object, Governor. I took a couple of instant pictures of the injuries. May we—so to speak— put them in to evidence?
Laura Certainly.

Probyn takes a card from Dr Graham to the desk where she, Laura and Frances look at it. Dr Graham hands one to the Rev. John

Rev. John I find this dreadful.
Dr Graham Nonsense. Could have been much worse. She obviously broke away quickly. (*She lights another cigarette*)
Rev. John I mean the humiliation. Being photographed.
Dr Graham My dear man, d'you think you've a monopoly of pity? I fed her sleeping pills and took 'em while she was flat out.
Rev. John I humbly apologize.
Dr Graham No need. But keep your spiritual toes under the table. The way I feel about this, I'm almost bound to tread on 'em.
Laura Doctor, can you tell us anything more from these?
Dr Graham I'm no detective, if that's what you mean. But I'd say there were three or perhaps five blows. With something narrow. And flattish and fairly flexible.
Frances A belt?
Dr Graham No-o. I shouldn't think so. The bruises suggest something harder. If you look at the edges of the weals . . .
Probyn It must have been a gardening tool of some kind.
Dr Graham Probably, but I can't think what. A broom handle—any kind of handle—would be more rounded.
Probyn We searched, naturally. Everything was cleaned and in place.
Frances It would be, wouldn't it? That's the obvious thing they'd think of.
Laura Well, we've a little more detail. What did you say, Doctor—(*she makes a note on a pad*)—narrow, flat, flexible.
Dr Graham And possibly about three feet long.

Laura tears off the note and gives it to Marian

Laura Ring Miss Barnes. Give her this information and tell them to go on looking. It must be somewhere.

Marian makes the telephone call without interrupting the dialogue

Dr Graham You know, there's something about these pictures. I can't place it. I've a feeling I've seen something before. (*She smites her forehead*) My damned memory.

Rev. John We've so little to work on. What happens if we reach an *impasse?*

Laura We call in an official investigator.

Frances And it becomes a police matter.

Laura I want to avoid that. We get an atmosphere of sullenness and resentment which can last for weeks.

Frances Then whoever knows must be made to speak.

Dr Graham Penalize the lot of 'em and be done with it.

Laura I couldn't do that.

Frances Why not?

Laura It would be impracticable and unjust.

Rev. John The innocent suffering for the guilty.

Dr Graham They're all here because they're guilty of something. Not speaking makes them accessories and guilty of that much more.

Laura Rather spurious reasoning, don't you think?

Dr Graham Well, we won't solve this by being scrupulous.

Rev. John The Governor is right. It would be unjust.

Dr Graham Now look, Rev. John, loving kindness is all very well, but how many of them know the meaning of it?

Rev. John ⌈ We need to set an example . . .

Frances ⟨ But if we're to get anywhere at all . . .

Probyn ⌊ If I may be allowed to suggest . . .

Laura If you please.

They subside

We shan't get anywhere by arguing amongst ourselves.

Rev. John I'm sorry. I fear I was carried away.

Dr Graham My fault as usual. I speak too bluntly. I expect that's why they call me Forthright Fan.

Rev. John I didn't know you knew.

Dr Graham turns to him, but there is a knock at the main door

Laura I said we weren't to be disturbed. Chief, would you mind?

Probyn goes to the door. Collins is outside, and they speak

Dr Graham looks at the photo

Dr Graham I wish I could remember about this. I've got an idea it might be important.

Probyn Would you excuse me a moment, madam? It's relevant.

Laura Yes, Chief.

Probyn exits, shutting the door

Frances We're not making progress. Wouldn't it be best to refer what details we have and ask for instructions?

Laura That would make it official. I'd rather wait a bit longer.

Rev. John I wonder, now, would there be anything to gain by having a word with Marcy?

Laura Marcy? She's the last person to give anyone away.

Rev. John Not directly. But she has a lot of freedom. She pops up all over the place. And she's very loquacious. She might let something drop. Quite inadvertently.

Laura We could try. Though personally I think . . .

Probyn enters with a longish thin object wrapped in sacking

Probyn I think we have the weapon.

They all stand up. Probyn puts the package on the desk

One of the men found it and brought it in.

Laura pulls aside the covering to reveal a long piece of wood

Laura Where was it found?

Probyn Hidden in the hedge. That's why he was suspicious. It's from the shed pulled down recently. He said it wasn't there yesterday.

Laura What do you think, Doctor?

Probyn takes the package to the table. Dr Graham examines it

Dr Graham Very likely. Look—one end's broken. Could be when she got away.

A whistle blows outside. Probyn glances at her watch

Frances It could be finger-printed. But only if we call in the police and you don't want . . .

Laura No.

Frances So what next?

Laura We'll speak to Marcy. If that fails, I'll make a last appeal to Kate . . .

The whistle blows again. Probyn looks up sharply and stands looking over at the windows

Rev. John When I saw her yesterday, she was adamant. I don't suppose it matters if I tell you—after all, we're not exactly under the seal of the confessional, but she did say if we pressed this too far we might regret it.

The whistle blows again—this time three short blasts. Probyn runs to the windows and looks out

Laura Whatever happens won't be pleasant. I think we must be prepared to . . .

Probyn (*suddenly*) Madam, there seems to be something wrong down there.

Laura Wrong?

Probyn They are not obeying the whistle. They are standing still in their lines.

They all move to the windows and look down

Frances What's the matter with them, for heaven's sake?

Probyn I'd better get down there.

Probyn exits quickly, shutting the door behind her

Laura Who is that speaking to Miss Barnes?

Frances It looks like—yes, it is. Valentine.

Laura Valentine. (*She sits at her desk*)

Dr Graham There seems to be an argument going on.

Laura Miss Oates, get Valentine's record. (*She gives Marian her keys from the drawer*)

Marian goes to the filing cabinet. Laura resumes work

Rev. John She's gone back into line.

The whistle sounds the three short blasts

Frances They're still not obeying. Ah—here comes the Chief.

Dr Graham I hope she gives 'em hell. I know that Valentine. A crafty devil. Always has an answer. Preferably insolent.

Marian brings Laura a folder

Frances What's she in for?

Laura Demonstrating, principally.

Rev. John That's not, in itself, a prison offence.

Laura Not to start with. She just went on and on. (*She runs her finger down the page*) Ban the Bomb, Vietnam. And not always political, either. This and that and the other. Quite a list.

Frances (*looking over Laura's shoulder*) You name it, she sat down on it.

Rev. John What made them put her inside?

Laura They seem to have been lenient at first. Fined. Fined again. About a dozen times. (*Turning a page*) Ah, she seems to have widened her scope. Inciting to violence. A brick through an embassy window.

Dr Graham That old suffragist stuff? And they think they're so up to date.

Laura The magistrates finally lost patience and decided to teach her a lesson.

Frances So we got her. Why haven't we thought of her in connection with Kate?

Laura What reason? As far as I can see, she hasn't indulged in personal violence. Apart from resisting arrest.

Dr Graham You disappoint me. Hasn't she even bitten a policeman?

Laura (*smiling*) If she has, there's no official record. (*She closes the file*)

Probyn enters

Probyn (*grimly*) Madam . . .

They all turn

We appear to have a strike on our hands.
Frances A strike!
Laura Why?
Probyn They won't say. They want you to see their representative.
Laura (*nodding*) Valentine.
Probyn Yes. I am to say that unless you agree to what they say, they will stay outside indefinitely.
Frances An ultimatum.
Probyn They would like to think so.
Frances Shall I speak to them?
Laura No. Chief, go back and tell them that I accept no ultimatums and I make no conditions. They are all to return to their rooms at once. Quietly. No protests. No demonstrations. Then, and only then, I'll hear what Valentine has to say.
Probyn And if they still refuse to move?
Laura They may do as they said. Remain there indefinitely. All outside doors will be locked. Is that clear?
Probyn Yes, madam. (*She turns to go*)
Laura And, Chief . . .
Probyn Yes, madam?
Laura You may also tell them I have all the patience in the world. And they have all the time.
Probyn (*grimly*) Right.

Probyn marches out, closing the door

Dr Graham Stupid fools. They know they can't get away with it.
Rev. John Whatever it is, they must feel very strongly.
Laura I imagine Valentine has worked them up.
Frances Can it be to do with Kate?
Laura We'll know in due course. Miss Oates, let me see your notes.

Laura and Marian discuss the notes. The others look out of the windows

Frances They might stay there all night.
Laura That's their affair.
Frances This place is not enclosed. Some of them might break away.
Laura How far do you think they will get? In prison uniform. With no money.
Frances Shouldn't we be prepared to compromise?
Laura No. (*She speaks to Marian aside*)
Rev. John There's something unnerving about mass quietude. Far more effective than hysteria. Look, they're standing like stones.
Dr Graham Better than throwing them.
Frances They're listening to the Chief.
Laura Please would you come away from the windows. It's better at this stage to seem uninterested.

Dr Graham and Rev. John go back to their chairs. Frances comes to Laura

Frances Don't you think we should . . .
Laura Just a moment. (*She speaks to Marian*)

Marian goes and looks in the top drawer of the cabinet

 (*Quietly*) Sit down, Frances.
Frances But . . .
Laura Sit down. (*She starts to write*)

Frances sits, tapping restlessly with a pencil. The Rev. John gestures at her and she stops. Dr Graham strikes a match. The whistle blows three sharp blasts. They all look over to the windows. There is a tense silence. Everyone is still. Only Laura goes on writing unmoved. Suddenly the marching is heard. Everyone relaxes. Marian shuts the filing cabinet. Dr Graham's match burns her fingers. Her exclamation finally breaks the silence. The marching grows louder, and then fades out. Frances gets up

Frances What now? Send for Valentine?

Laura takes off her spectacles and looks up, smiling

Laura There's no immediate hurry. We'll have a break for tea.

Laura reaches for the intercom, as—

the CURTAIN *falls*

SCENE 2

The same. Half an hour later

As the CURTAIN rises, the rattle of teacups and sound of conversation is heard from the inner room. Collins is standing against the main door with Valentine by her side. Valentine is twenty-four, a handsome and obvious rebel, with an irrepressible sense of wickedness and a sideways glinting glance. She has style, even her uniform has been shaped by its belt to fit her figure. After a second, she shifts impatiently from one foot to the other

Valentine For God's sake—what're they doing in there? We've been waiting twenty minutes.
Collins And we shall wait for another twenty if necessary. So stand still and be quiet.
Valentine (*politely*) Pardon me while I breathe.
Collins That will do.

Valentine stands still. Then she digs Collins in the ribs

Valentine Do you suppose they're having it off with the parson?
Collins Quiet!

Valentine (*laughing*) Poor old basket—three dried-up spinsters and a widow past it . . .
Collins I shan't warn you again.

Valentine glaces sideways, smiling. She stands still again for a second, then breaks into song

Valentine "We shall not be moved. . . ."
Collins One more word from you . . .

Valentine makes a sweeping gesture and runs forward, looking into the audience. Collins follows her

Valentine And I want you all to get right out of your seats and come up here . . .

Laughing, Valentine runs round the desk with Collins after her. She ends up in her original position, hands at her sides

You cannot touch me, for I am saved. (*With a sideways glint*) Are you saved, Collins? Have you found the light?
Collins You'll see the light of the punishment room if you're not careful.
Valentine (*singing*) "The people's flag is deepest red . . ." (*She falters as the others file in from the inner room, then sings the next line defiantly*)

Collins pulls Valentine back against the door

Marian enters, followed by Frances, the Rev. John, Dr Graham and Probyn. Laura comes last

They all stand by their original seats until Laura has sat at her desk then they too sit. Collins moves Valentine down in front of the desk and steps back by the door. Laura opens Valentine's folder

Laura (*quietly*) You have quite a good voice, Valentine. Have you ever used it apart from these demonstrations?
Valentine (*slightly thrown*) Ma'am . . .
Laura You might have organized a choir here. That would have at least been creative. This record shows only a misguided ability for destruction.
Valentine (*sullenly*) I am not on report, madam.
Laura Not yet. So what is it you have to say to me?
Valentine Speaking as the elected representative of the people . . .
Laura (*crisply*) The elected representative of the people is either a Member of Parliament or the President of the United States. Which are you at this particular moment?
Valentine You are making fun of me.
Laura Then stop this ridiculous play-acting, and use simple English.
Valentine On behalf of the community I have been asked to speak to you . . .
Laura By whom? Be specific.
Valentine (*hesitating*) Why—I . . .

Laura Who originally approached you with this request? Or have you taken the whole issue on yourself?

Valentine Someone has to speak against injustice.

Laura And what is this injustice?

Valentine This enquiry. It must be stopped.

Laura Why?

Valentine Walmer was punished by the will of the people . . .

Laura Who are not to be punished in turn?

Valentine That is the position, ma'am.

Laura It is not tenable and you know it. If this is all you have to say, you are wasting my time and your own.

Valentine You sent a message you were prepared to listen. It is our right to ask to see you.

Laura Yes. Have you anything more to say?

Valentine This enquiry is to stop. Until we have your agreement, no more work will be done. Of any kind. By any one of us.

Laura Now listen to me, Valentine. Did you personally attack Walmer?

Valentine No.

Collins coughs meaningly

Madam.

Laura But obviously you know who did.

Valentine Of course, madam.

Laura And why should this person—or persons—be protected?

Valentine If you uncover the truth, you will be sorry.

Laura You may not threaten, Valentine. Or is that a statement?

Valentine Neither, madam. A protest.

Laura You have been making protests for years. And where has it got you? Here.

Valentine I have proved I will suffer for a cause.

Laura Nonsense. If you want to reform the world it's your privilege to try. Screaming, shouting and damaging property is not the answer.

Valentine The Suffragettes . . .

Laura Did not gain the franchise by militancy. Do your homework. One day you should look up the records and see how many recent acts have been passed through the proper channels. With intelligence and dignity.

Valentine It takes too long . . .

Laura Are your methods any quicker? No, Valentine, you're not a reformer. Not a martyr. You're a bore.

Valentine (*stung and furious*) A bore!

Laura Yes—you and others like you. Irritating, time-wasting bores. All you want is the limelight.

Valentine Madam . . .

Laura You have deliberately used this enquiry to ferment trouble and bring yourself to the fore.

Valentine I came to speak to you . . .

Laura You have made all your points. This enquiry will continue. While you are shut in your room like the others, you will have time to think. Take a long cool look at yourself. Miss Collins . . .

Collins opens the door. Valentine starts to march out. Laura turns to give Marian the folder, speaking rather more kindly, with her back to Valentine

And for heaven's sake, you silly girl, do as I say. Otherwise you may find yourself in serious trouble.

Valentine (*turning*) Trouble? (*She laughs shortly*) Not me, madam. I'm on the pill.

Collins shuts the door. Laura turns. Dr Graham exclaims. The Rev. John stops her

Laura (*gently*) Figuratively speaking, of course.

Valentine Oh, not in here. I mean—who's available? Unless . . . (*She glints sideways to the Rev. John—something between a leer and an invitation, lewd and quite horrible*)

Probyn jumps up and moves to one side of Valentine, Collins to the other. The Rev. John and Dr Graham both move slightly. Laura's voice cuts in. Instinctively, Valentine comes to attention

Laura Valentine! (*She is very quiet, very measured*) You will go and stand in front of the chaplain. And you will apologize.

Valentine (*trying wide-eyed innocence*) What for, ma'am?

Laura (*still quietly*) You will do as I say. At once. That is an order.

Valentine faces her. She moves to the desk, places her hands on it, and leans across. Collins and Probyn seize her

Valentine No.

Laura Leave her.

Probyn and Collins step back

Very well. You may remain in that uncomfortable position for precisely two minutes. Then Miss Collins and the Chief Officer will remove you forcibly. And I shall personally see that you lose your remission.

Valentine You can't do . . .

Laura (*crisply*) Two minutes. (*She glances deliberately at her watch, then gets up and stands at the window with her back to the room*)

There is a long pause, during which Collins and Probyn exchange a glance and step back slightly. Valentine straightens up. She goes and stands stiffly before the Rev. John. He gets up

Valentine (*woodenly*) Sir. The Governor wishes me to apologize.

Rev. John (*quietly*) Thank you, Valentine. (*He moves down by the file stands with his back to the room*)

Collins About turn. Back to the Governor's desk. Smartly there.

Valentine walks rigidly back to the desk. Laura returns from the windows

Laura Take her away, please, Miss Collins.

Collins opens the door. Probyn returns to her chair

Collins (*crisply*) Out!

Valentine marches defiantly out. She begins to sing "The Red Flag" again. It is taken up by distant voices off. Collins follows, closing the door

A whistle blows three blasts. The singing trails off to silence

Laura The waste—the wicked senseless waste of intelligence.

Frances (*uncertain*) Governor—did you really need to pulp her like that?

Laura I found I could not help myself. After all these years I am still shaken by evil.

Rev. John Come—not evil. Perhaps—misguided?

Dr Graham Misbegotten!

Laura (*abruptly*) She had done all this to cover up something. Now I wonder . . .

There is a knock on the main door

I said we were not to be disturbed. Marian—

Probyn I'll go. (*She half opens the door and stands speaking to someone outside*)

The dialogue continues without a break

Laura I apologize again for that incident, Padre. It was quite inexcusable insolence.

Rev. John My dear Governor, it's an occupational hazard. I once had a twelve-stone shoplifter spit with devastating accuracy into my right eye.

Dr Graham (*interestedly*) You turned the other cheek?

Rev. John Alas—she was removed before I could exercise that privilege. (*He sits again*)

Probyn closes the door and comes into the room

Laura Nothing important, Chief?

Probyn Only Marcy. Asking to collect the teacups. I told her it must wait.

Laura Thank you.

Frances Quite suddenly I'm tired of Marcy and her everlasting crockery. She scurries in and out like a waitress at a hotel.

Laura Like a . . . (*Suddenly*) Indeed, she does. Chief, would you fetch her back, please?

Probyn Now, madam?

Laura Now. (*She nods at Probyn*)

Probyn exits

Frances Why?

Laura Don't you see the significance?

Frances Sig . . .

Dr Graham (*grimly*) Yes, Governor. Yes, indeed.

*Probyn enters with Marcy. She speaks aside, motioning to the inner room.
Marcy ducks her head and scurries off into it. Probyn resumes her seat*

Frances (*suddenly*) Oh, yes, I see. Sorry to be so dim. By the way, Governor, there's one other thing, if I may . . .
Laura Yes?
Frances You definitely intend to put them all—the whole community—on dietary punishment?
Laura Certainly.
Frances That means that everyone must be examined by Dr Graham. It'll be rather a long job.
Dr Graham (*grimly*) Believe me, it'll be a pleasure.

Marcy enters with a tray of cups and moves to the main door

Laura Marcy . . .
Marcy Yes, Governor dear?
Laura Put the tray down. Over there—on the table.
Marcy Ma'am?

Probyn snaps her fingers to attract Marcy's attention and points to the alcove table. Marcy puts down the tray

Laura Come here, please.

Marcy goes to the desk

You may sit down.
Marcy Sit . . .
Laura In that chair.

Marcy looks round, puzzled, then sits as Laura has indicated, leaning forward apprehensively

Marcy I done nothing, Governor dear—honest. Not so much as a blinking dog-end . . .
Laura Why are you running around collecting cups?
Marcy Why—it's my job—'mongst other things.
Laura (*drily*) There appears to be a strike on.
Marcy Oh. That.
Laura Aren't you included?
Marcy W-e-ll, I . . .
Laura Yes, Marcy?
Marcy (*desperately*) I'm only on a go-slow.

The Rev. John hides an involuntary smile

Laura And what does that mean?
Marcy I gotter sort of—(*she glances quickly at the Rev. John*)—special dispensation. (*To Laura*) It's my age, you see.
Laura So what does this—go-slow—entail?

Marcy I finish up my work today, proper like. After that, I takes my own time.

Laura I see. And who told you to do this?

Marcy I wasn't exactly—told—ma'am.

Laura Where did you get your orders?

Marcy (*playing for time*) Ma'am?

Laura Stop playing possum, Marcy. You were not outside this morning when this happened. You did not stand in the lines. So you must have received your—er—instructions some other way.

Marcy claps her hand defensively to her pocket

So come along, Marcy.

Marcy I'm not getting anyone into trouble, Governor.

Laura The whole community is already in trouble. And that includes you.

Marcy slowly brings out a crumpled note and smoothes it out on her knee

Marcy I didn't want no striking, Governor dear. But I 'ad to go along with the others, didn't I? You do see.

Laura Give that to me, please.

Marcy reluctantly passes the note, which is now seen to be on toilet paper. Laura reads it

So. (*She hands it to Frances, then continues talking to Marcy*)

Frances reads the note, then passes it to Probyn, who also reads it with Dr Graham and the Rev. John

I take it everyone had these instructions?

Marcy Well, you know so much, it can't hurt now. Yes, they did.

Laura How were they passed round?

Marcy I'm not saying.

Laura (*quietly*) I think you'd better.

Marcy obstinately shakes her head

(*Sharply*) Marcy, this is enough. It was Valentine, wasn't it?

Marcy gulps, then nods, dumbly

And how did she deliver these notes?

Marcy In—in her little cart.

Frances and Marian react

You know how she goes round every day—with the laundry.

Frances (*suddenly*) That horrible little squeaking cart! To think of her calmly working all this out—and then—quite openly . . .

Laura (*aside*) Miss Treadgold!

Frances It is abominable.

Laura Marcy, listen to me—and carefully. I want you to tell me exactly how you spent yesterday morning.

Marcy Ma'am?

Laura Starting after breakfast.

Again Marcy hesitates. She glances over at the Rev. John

Marcy Padre, tell her I don't want to cause no more trouble.

Rev. John This isn't causing trouble, Marcy. You may be helping to shorten the punishment for the others.

Marcy Oh. (*She considers this*) Honest to God, sir?

Rev. John Honest to God, Marcy.

Marcy Thank you, sir. (*To Laura*) Well, after breakfast, I did my cleaning —office, Miss Treadgold, Chief—(*to Probyn*)—rare lot of papers you have lying around, Miss, if you don't mind my saying so——

Laura taps a pencil on the desk. Marcy turns

—and then, Miss Oates, she comes up and says: "Marcy, take these flowers and put them on the Governor's desk"—only I never did.

Frances (*abruptly*) Never did what?

Marcy Put them on the desk. Because as I was coming up the stairs, all hell broke loose—screaming and running—and there was Kate with them all behind her . . .

Laura Yes?

Marcy I waited a bit and let things get quieter.

Frances That's quite right. She came in while I was talking to the Chief.

Marcy Then Miss Treadgold, she said you get the hell out of here, Marcy, only—beg pardon, miss—she didn't say exactly that, but more or less, and I said I come to bring the flowers and she said just you skip off sharpish and get Gow to make some hot coffee.

Laura (*to Frances*) Correct?

Frances (*thoughtfully*) Yes. So far.

Laura So . . . ?

Marcy So like she said. I went down to the kitchen and made the coffee and brung it up smartly. That's when she give me a fag—(*confidentially*) —remember, I told you?

Laura Will you please forget about . . .

Frances suddenly gets up

Frances Marcy—Governor, would you mind?

Laura No.

Frances Marcy, did you make the coffee yourself?

Marcy Yes, miss.

Frances I specially asked for it to be made by Gow.

Marcy Gow wasn't in the kitchen then.

There is a general slight reaction

And you did say to me—move.

Laura Why was Gow not there?

Marcy She never is at that time. (*She stops dead. Her hand goes to her mouth. She looks round at them all*)

Laura Why?

Marcy She—she likes to go out after a bit of mint or 'erbs or something —you know what she is about her blooming flavours.
Laura Marcy.

Marcy stops again

Every day? At the same time?

Marcy looks round at them all again

Well?
Marcy But—surely you knew?
Laura About what?
Marcy Gow. And Valentine.
Laura (*rising*) Have you something rather important to tell us, Marcy?

Marcy stares at her. A look of horror crosses her face. She gets up. She stands at attention behind the chair

Marcy Permission to leave, madam.
Laura Permission refused. (*She is completely hard and official*)

The Chief moves beside Marcy

You will tell me exactly what you are talking about. Everything. And in detail. Understand?
Marcy (*beginning to break down*) I can't—I can't. I thought you knew—I thought everyone knew.
Laura Knew what?
Marcy No. You mustn't ask me. (*She turns blindly down to the Rev. John*)

Probyn holds her back

Padre—Padre—help me . . .

The Rev. John rises and moves towards her

Probyn (*quietly*) That will do.

Marcy breaks away to the Rev. John and catches his arm

Marcy Please, sir—please, sir . . .

The Rev. John puts an arm round Marcy's shoulders. He nods to Probyn, who stands back

Rev. John All right, Marcy. All right. Calm yourself. Here. (*He gives her a handkerchief*) That's better. (*To Laura*) One moment, Governor, please, I do beg you.

Laura nods and sits down. She speaks to Marian, who makes a telephone call

Now, Marcy, listen to me. You cannot draw back now.
Marcy I didn't know I'd make so much trouble.
Rev. John (*gently*) You owe it to us. And to your own conscience.
Marcy People—like me—aren't supposed to have no conscience.

Rev. John Come, that's nonsense. And it is not even a simple matter of conscience. It is a matter of duty. I told you this morning—remember? The Governor has been very good to you. It is now your duty to tell her all you know.

Marcy (*wiping her eyes*) If you think so, sir.

Rev. John I do, Marcy. And you know I am right. (*Gently*) Am I not right, Marcy?

Marcy (*very low*) I suppose so, sir.

Rev. John You must be sure, Marcy. Are you quite sure?

Marcy (*in almost a whisper*) Yes, sir.

Rev. John Thank you. (*He gives her hand a comforting clasp*) Now go back to the Governor's desk. (*He sits*)

Probyn takes Marcy to her chair. She sits, and Probyn stands behind her

Laura Finish what you have to tell me.

Marcy Gow and Valentine have a thing.

Laura A thing. (*It is not a question*)

Marcy About each other. (*She looks round at them*) But you must have known. Why do you think Gow is always rowing with cook?

Laura And what has Mrs Beatty to do with it?

Marcy She likes Val. Oh—not in that way. But you know how good Val is with a needle, and she does things for Mrs Beatty—she made her a dress in her spare time—and so Gow gets flaming jealous and takes it out on Mrs Beatty when they're in the kitchen—and a rare lot of old shindigs there are . . .

Laura Thank you, Marcy, and how often does this happen?

Marcy Meaning Gow and Val? Whenever they can meet. I mean—Gow slips out for 'er blooming 'erbs or some excuse. And Val's pretty free—round and about with her little cart . . .

Laura Very well, I understand.

Marcy (*suddenly*) Governor dear, I'm sorry. I really am. But it really isn't so bad—Val's a tough one but she won't be here much longer.

Laura That will do.

Marcy I only wanted to say when she's gone I don't reckon anyone else'll take her place—if you get me. And if that's any comfort to you . . .

Laura (*smiling*) Thank you, Marcy.

There is a knock on the main door

Come in.

Collins enters

Collins You sent for me, madam.

Laura Yes, please wait a moment. (*To Marcy*) One last question—do you know where Gow and Valentine meet?

Marcy Here and there, according to where they are. But most of the times it's over in Reception—it's not locked and it's warm with them pipes . . .

Laura Do you happen to know if they were there yesterday morning?

Marcy I couldn't be sure. But I was shaking me duster out of the window and I did see the little cart . . .
Laura Near the Reception wing?
Marcy Propped agin the end door.
Laura Thank you. (*To Collins*) Take her back to her room.

Without interrupting the dialogue, Probyn sits. Marcy stands with her back to the audience discussing something with the Rev. John and Probyn

She will share the punishment with the others.
Collins About that, madam. It is time for their tea.
Laura Carry on as usual. Normal meals will be served until I have made final arrangements with Dr Graham.
Collins Very good, madam. (*She opens the door*)
Marcy (*going to the desk*) Please, Governor . . .
Laura What is it?
Marcy If you could—not say who told you . . .
Laura It will not be necessary.
Marcy Thank Gawd. (*She goes to the door, giving a quick thumbs-up sign as she passes the table. In the doorway she pauses*) Governor dear, you're a real gent.

Marcy exits: Collins follows, closing the door

Dr Graham Well, well. So that's all it was. (*She reaches for another cigarette*)
Rev. John (*drily*) Just a puff of smoke. (*He strikes a match for her*)
Dr Graham My dear good man, it's forty years since I was a wide-eyed innocent. This is routine. Here—give me that before you burn your fingers. (*She takes the lighted match for her cigarette*)
Laura It is not a criminal offence and they cannot be punished for it.
Frances You'll separate them.
Laura Of course.
Frances And all this jealousy, and the fighting in the kitchen . . .
Laura Gow has already been taken off kitchen duty. I may have to make that permanent. Such a pity. She can work so well when she likes.
Dr Graham What about Valentine? Inciting the others to mutiny . . .
Laura She will be punished with the rest of them. There is no need to be more harsh with her than anyone else.
Dr Graham You're too lenient. The sheer calculating arrogance—provoking a strike as a smoke screen for this . . .
Laura (*smiling*) You can't say she didn't warn us.
Dr Graham Are you by any chance offering that in mitigation?
Rev. John My dear Janet, I beg you will not start another fight.
Frances (*breaking in*) I foresee a series of fights in dealing with Gow. She's difficult enough in the normal way.
Dr Graham Normal? The poor devil's sick.
Frances You know what I mean. Excitable. Always shouting and waving her arms about.
Laura (*abruptly*) Yes. (*She sits back in her chair, obviously thinking*)

Dr Graham I agree with the Governor. This is ordinary everyday stuff and she'll cope with it without fuss.

Frances But we still haven't solved the main problem. This enquiry has uncovered something unexpected. It hasn't brought us any nearer knowing who beat up Kate.

Probyn Isn't that obvious now? With Marcy's evidence?

Frances They will deny it absolutely. We have no way to prove it.

Laura (*suddenly*) Maybe we have.

They all look at her

Frances Why—do you think . . .

Laura May I see those photographs again?

Dr Graham Surely. Here. (*She blows cigarette ash off the photos and gives them to Probyn*)

Probyn takes the photos to the desk and she, Laura and Frances look at them. Dr Graham smiles at the Rev. John

Sorry, Rev. John, I seem to be provoking you more than usual. You'll have to excommunicate me.

Rev. John (*drily*) It's hardly necessary. When did I last see you at early service?

Dr Graham If we get this business settled without bloodshed, you shall see me six times running. And that's a promise.

Laura Doctor—(*she takes the photographs to the table and fans them out*) —will you look at these again?

Frances and Probyn follow Laura

Dr Graham Certainly. Why?

Laura You said something puzzled you.

Dr Graham It still does.

Laura Is it possible that those blows were made—by someone left-handed?

Dr Graham By God—(*to the Rev. John*)—and that's not blasphemy—let me look. Wait now. (*She puts on her spectacles*) So. Let's see. I've already said I'm not a detective, but . . .

Laura Just give me your opinion.

Dr Graham examines the photos

Well?

Dr Graham Don't rush me. You may be on to something. On the other hand—Miss Oates, have you got a ruler handy?

Marian looks for a ruler on the desk

Now, obviously whoever did this beating stood squarely behind and not at the side. The weals are too vertical.

Marian brings a ruler to Dr Graham

Thanks. So—(*she places the ruler on the photographs as though it were the weapon*)—if she stood like that—and used her right arm—the welts would go that way. And with her left hand, that way . . . (*She throws down the ruler and removes her spectacles*) Governor, I believe—mind, I'm not one hundred per cent sure—but I do believe you have it.

Laura Show me again. With the ruler.

Dr Graham So—for the—here, wait. Chief . . . (*Still sitting, she turns Probyn with her back to the audience. She demonstrates the angle of the ruler on Probyn's back as she talks*) So—for the right hand. So—for the left. (*Throwing down the ruler*) Dammit, who's talking about a hundred per cent. It *has* to be like that.

Laura goes to her desk

Laura Chief.

Probyn Madam?

Laura (*crisply*) First get Miss Collins. Then bring over Kate.

Dr Graham Kate?

Laura (*to Probyn*) I want Kate, Valentine and Gow.

Probyn Separately or . . .

Laura Together. Line them up here—in front of the desk.

Probyn Now, madam?

Laura (*firmly*) Now.

As Probyn goes out quickly through the main door—

the CURTAIN *falls*

ACT III

The same. Five minutes later

The chair below the desk has been removed. The piece of wood in its canvas wrap lies on the floor between Marian's chair and the desk

As the CURTAIN *rises, Frances, Dr Graham, the Rev. John, Marian and Laura are round the table looking at the photographs and discussing them. The telephone rings, and Marian goes to answer it*

Marian Governor's office.

Dr Graham I tell you there's no doubt about it.

Frances Surely—a certain amount of supposition . . .

Dr Graham Oh, supposition my foot.

Marian Excuse me, madam—

Laura turns

—it's Reception. Kate's husband is here.

Laura Walmer? Why?

Marian It's his routine visit. He was sent over to the hospital. But Kate's on her way here.

Laura He shouldn't have been sent to the hospital without reference to me.

Marian He hasn't been told anything. He's a bit disturbed.

Rev. John Well, of course, poor fellow. Shall I see him?

Laura Not for the moment. I want this situation completely cleared up first.

Rev. John But we can't leave him in suspense.

Laura No, no. Miss Oates, have him brought up here—the little waiting-room opposite will do. Ask—let's see, we don't want to be too official. Who's available from the officers—someone tactful and reassuring?

Rev. John I think Mrs Mayhew should be here.

Marian Yes, sir. Friday *is* her day.

Laura Good. Get through to her and arrange it, will you, please. Ask him to accept my apologies for delay and say I hope to see him very shortly.

Marian Yes, madam.

Laura And stress that Kate isn't ill. Stress that particularly. If she could give the impression all this is a matter of routine . . .

Marian Yes, madam. (*She speaks into the telephone*)

Marching feet are heard in the corridor

Probyn (*off*) Smartly there. Wait by the door. Gow, straighten up.

The footsteps stop

Probyn knocks and enters, holding the door open

Walmer, Valentine and Gow, Madam.

Laura Bring them in.

Probyn opens the door wide and stands by it

Probyn (*calling*) Miss Collins.

Collins moves across the open doorway and stands facing the way she came

Collins Forward!

Gow, Valentine and Kate march in (in that order)

Probyn (*as they enter*) Up here, please. Before the desk. In line. Hands behind your back and face the Governor.

Collins comes in last and stands behind Valentine

Probyn shuts the door and moves to top end of desk. Collins moves back against the door. Frances sits at the top end of table. Rev. John centre. Dr. Graham at lower end. Marian opens her notebook

Laura I'm asking you for the last time. Has anyone anything to tell me?

No-one answers

Kate?

Kate (*quietly*) No, ma'am.

Laura Gow?

Gow shrugs

Probyn (*sharply*) Answer the Governor.

Gow No, madam.

Laura Valentine?

Valentine No further comment.

Collins coughs warningly

Valentine Ma'am.

Laura Very well. (*She turns to give Marian a note, then speaks casually, with her back to the girls*) Have you always been left-handed, Gow?

Frances, Dr Graham and the Rev. John react

Gow (*puzzled*) Yes, ma'am.

Laura I thought so. When you destroyed my flowers yesterday, you used your left hand.

Gow What's that got to do with anything . . .

Laura (*turning*) Kate was beaten by a left-handed person. No—no more denials or arguments.

Valentine Why should . . .
Laura (*cutting her short*) And you, Valentine, will do well not to interrupt. We know that you and Gow got Kate into the Reception Block and assaulted her. We know what with.

Marian hands Laura the stick from the floor. Laura puts it on the desk

Don't tell me you have never seen that before. (*She looks at them*)

They remain silent

Now—are you going to tell me why you did it?

No-one answers

Then I will tell you. Because Kate killed her child.
Gow What! (*She goes into wild hysterical laughter*)

Collins darts down and holds Gow. Dr Graham gets up. Valentine moves, but Probyn grabs her

Valentine Gow—you fool!
Dr Graham Quiet, girl! Control yourself.
Gow (*screaming*) A kid—a bloody kid! Who cares!
Valentine (*struggling with Probyn*) It was because of the child—tell them it was because of the child . . .
Gow (*screaming*) It wasn't even *human* . . . !

Dr Graham slaps Gow's face. She screams loudly and falls with her face towards the footlights. She shouts and beats her hands frantically on the floor. Laura runs across and helps Dr Graham to hold her

Dr Graham (*over her shoulder, to the Rev. John*) I need room—clear those chairs . . .

Dr Graham and Laura struggle with Gow. The Rev. John passes the three chairs, one by one, to Collins, who puts them through the inner door. Then he pushes the table back against the bookcase. Frances takes Kate to the window-seat, where they sit. Valentine struggles with Probyn who holds her firmly above the desk. None of this interrupts the dialogue

Valentine Let me go to her! Please!

Gow raises herself on her hands and screams across at Valentine

Gow I told you I'd do it. You should have left those bitches alone!
Dr Graham That's enough. On your feet.

Dr Graham and Laura get Gow up. She resists, half-crouched between them, still shouting across at Valentine

Gow I saw you. First Beatty, then Walmer. Smiling at them, pawing them . . .
Valentine No, Gow—no! You imagined it.
Gow I ought to kill you! (*She breaks from Dr Graham and Laura and launches herself at Valentine*)

Collins runs in just in time to grab Gow

You *bitch*! (*She spits at Valentine, screams again, and breaks from Collins, then she twists on her heel and collapses, head down stage*)

The Rev. John catches her and lowers her to the floor. Dr Graham kneels down. Laura backs to the desk

Dr Graham That's it, then. (*She feels Gow's pulse and looks quickly at her eyes*)

Gow lies still. Dr Graham gets up

Take her in the other room. All right, Governor?
Laura Yes. (*She sits at her desk*)

Dr Graham nods to Collins and the Rev. John

Collins and the Rev. John lift Gow between them and support her to the inner room. Dr Graham goes to the desk

Dr Graham Will you get the hospital, please? (*She lights a cigarette*)
Laura Miss Oates . . .

Marian dials a number

Is this a breakdown? Or just hysteria?
Dr Graham Looks like a breakdown. Probably been coming on for some time.
Laura We should have noticed.
Dr Graham You did notice.
Laura But . . .
Dr Graham You put it down to congenital bad temper. Now—don't start blaming yourself, or anyone else. You're not the first to be fooled by symptoms. (*She takes the telephone Marian hands to her*) Thanks. (*Into the phone*) Hullo . . . Yes. I've got another customer for you. Gow . . . Yes. Send a chair over, will you? The Governor's office. And I'd better have about three c.c.'s of . . . (*She goes on speaking inaudibly into the phone*)
Laura (*to Marian*) We shall need four copies of the notes. I'll tell you what to take next.
Marian Yes, madam.
Dr Graham (*putting down the phone*) Right. Now we'll get this over in short order.

Dr Graham exits to the inner room

Laura Valentine. Over here, please.

Valentine, now considerably subdued, moves in front of the desk. Probyn stands behind her

Valentine Madam—she can't help it. She's sick.

Laura Does that mean you're sick, too?
Valentine Not basically. I—I do it for kicks. But Gow—this may not be on her record. I think you ought to know.
Laura Yes? (*She nods to Marian to take notes*)
Valentine It happened when she was very young. About seventeen. There was a man. She was very fond of him. He lived on her earnings.
Laura Go on.
Valentine Well, she got older, you see, and she didn't do so well for him. So he got rid of her. And it did something to her. She has dreams—fantasies—she tells me. She needs someone to tell. In a way, I keep her sane.
Laura You do know you should have spoken about this?
Valentine I didn't want her to be put away. We'd got too involved.
Laura Emotionally.
Valentine Yes.
Laura When did that actually start?
Valentine Just after I came here. It was all right at first—(*a touch of the old defiance returns*)—well, dammit, it's not a criminal offence.

Probyn touches Valentine's arm warningly

Laura It was criminally stupid in your present circumstances. And then I suppose the trouble started? The jealousy—
Valentine Yes.
Laura —over Mrs Beatty.
Valentine Oh, we settled that. The real trouble was Kate.

Frances looks up

Kate Madam . . .

There is a knock on the main door

Laura Presently, Kate. Chief . . .

Probyn goes to the main door, speaks to someone not seen, then goes out, shutting the door behind her

You were saying?
Valentine It was a stupid mistake. I ran into Kate with my cart—accidentally—she wasn't looking where she was going. Well, I helped her up and brushed her down—we were laughing actually—it was all quite friendly. But Gow saw us. (*She pauses and glances over at Kate*) She thought I fancied Kate. She made an awful scene. She said she'd beat Kate to within an inch of her life.

Probyn enters carrying a kidney dish with cotton wool and a syringe

Probyn Excuse me, madam, they've sent the chair. And this is for the doctor.
Laura nods

Probyn goes into the inner room

(*To Valentine*) So?

Valentine Yesterday, I saw Gow speak to Kate and they slipped over to Reception.

Kate She said they had a letter for me.

Valentine I got over there quick. Gow knocked Kate down and started to hit her. I—well, I had to clout Gow. Then I grabbed Kate by the arm and told her to get the hell out of it.

Laura Kate—

Kate gets up and moves by Valentine

Probyn returns and stands by the two prisoners

—is all this correct?

Kate Yes, madam.

Laura Then I hope you both realize how foolishly you have behaved. (*To Valentine*) Did you honestly believe you'd get away with that strike idea?

Valentine It was worth a try. (*Sparking up for another second*) Well, I had to do something . . .

Dr Graham puts her head in

Dr Graham Governor . . .

Laura Yes, Doctor?

Dr Graham Is it all right to . . . ?

Laura Give me a moment.

Dr Graham withdraws her head

Valentine, you may go back to your room. I can't overlook this, of course. I'll deal with you later.

Valentine What about Gow, madam?

Laura She'll be taken good care of. No—you won't see her again.

Valentine But if I could . . .

Laura No. Chief.

Probyn takes Valentine's arm

Leave Walmer for the moment.

Probyn takes Valentine to the door and opens it for her to pass. Valentine pauses in the doorway

Valentine (*bitterly*) How the hell can you understand? You're so secure.

Valentine exits. Probyn follows, closing the door

Laura Please, Frances.

Frances opens the inner door

Frances All right now, Doctor. (*She remains by the door*)

Dr Graham enters. She goes to the main door and opens it wide, standing back and holding it open.
The Rev. John and Collins enter supporting Gow between them. She is semi-conscious, her head lolling in front of her, her legs trailing behind. They take her across and out by the main door

Dr Graham closes the door and turns to Laura

Dr Graham Let you have my report in the morning. Soon enough?
Laura Thank you.
Dr Graham Been quite a day, hasn't it?

Dr Graham goes out by the main door, closing it

Laura (*to Marian*) I think that'll be all for now. Type up what you can and leave the rest till tomorrow.
Marian Thank you, ma'am.

Marian gathers up her papers and exits by the main door, saying good night to Frances as she passes

Laura (*rising*) Kate, sit down, will you.

Laura brings chair from top end of desk to below desk

Kate sits. Laura indicates to Frances to move out of Kate's hearing

Go over and see the husband. Mrs Mayhew will have done her best, but she doesn't have the facts. When you've explained I'll see him in here.
Frances Do we tell him everything?
Laura Everything except the window business. And make it absolutely clear Kate isn't harmed.
Frances Right.

Frances goes out by the main door

Laura Now, Kate, no more shilly-shallying. I want to be sure there is nothing more on your mind.
Kate (*quietly*) No, madam. Why should there be?
Laura Because in my opinion none of it justifies your action yesterday.
Kate (*slowly*) I never—intended to jump.
Laura Yet you told me categorically you wanted to die.
Kate For the moment, I think I did. You see, I . . .
Laura For goodness' sake, girl, explain yourself.
Kate Those two poor creatures—it was all so humiliating. I couldn't bear

to be touched—by anyone. All I knew was to run, anywhere. Blindly. And the officers were behind me. So I said, "Don't touch me, or I'll jump." I'm sorry, madam. Everything seemed to—to pile up all at once. I've made a proper mess of things.

Laura Well, it's over now. (*She sits at her desk*) And I have some news for you. Your husband is here.

Kate Tom . . .

Laura It's his routine visit—yes, you're going to see him. Miss Treadgold is explaining to him now. But when you do see him, no self-reproaches, Kate. And no hysteria. We've had enough drama for one day.

Kate Madam—about Valentine and Gow.

Laura Well?

Kate Must they be punished?

Laura Why not?

Kate They're as they are. They can't help it.

Laura That's the oldest excuse in the book, Kate. And the weakest. Have you thought—just for a moment—what would happen if it were universally accepted?

Kate (*slowly*) We might have a kinder world.

Laura We'd have social chaos. And that would be only the beginning.

Tom enters by the main door without knocking. Frances is behind him, protesting

Frances Mr Walmer—wait—you can't . . .

Tom Kate . . .

Tom and Kate go into each other's arms

Frances I couldn't stop him. He already knows.

Tom It's true, then? You've been . . .

Kate No, Tom. Please . . .

Tom Is it true?

Kate Tom—the Governor . . .

Tom turns to Laura, still holding Kate close with one arm. He is about Kate's age, but does not have her strength of character. He wears formal clothes

Tom I beg your pardon, but I've been waiting. They told me nothing was wrong—but all that screaming in here—and then that woman came . . .

Laura Sit down, Mr Walmer.

Tom I have to know about my wife!

Kate Tom, it's all right.

Tom Let her answer me.

Laura I sent two of my staff to reassure you . . .

Tom (*almost incoherent*) First I'm sent to the hospital—then some woman brings me here and tells me a soothing tale and tells me to wait. Then this other woman . . .

Laura Miss Treadgold is the Assistant Governor.

Tom No—that little one they call Marcy—she brought me a cup of tea and she said, "If they tell you Kate's been beat up, it don't amount to anything . . ."

Laura Marcy . . .

Tom I want to know the truth!

Laura Yes, Mr Walmer. Unfortunately your wife was attacked, but if you will allow me—it is not serious . . .

Tom Not serious? Oh, my God, you say that—to me . . .

Kate Tom . . .

Tom Kate attacked—by some filthy—Kate who shouldn't be here . . .

Laura Mr Walmer, will you please sit down.

Tom sits. Kate puts her hand on his shoulder

Tom I've been weak—weak and wicked—but not any longer. We'll have the truth—all of it.

Kate (*urgently*) Tom—be careful!

Tom It's too late for that.

Kate (*desperately*) Madam, please don't listen to him.

Laura Mr Walmer, I can see you are under an emotional strain. Whatever it is you wish to tell me, perhaps you should think first.

Tom I've thought long enough.

Kate Oh—please . . .

Tom No. (*He looks up at her*) My mind is made up. But please—go over there. If you're near me—it makes it more difficult.

Kate Tom . . .

Tom (*steadily*) I'm going to talk to the Governor. *Please*, Kate.

Laura Miss Treadgold, please take Kate into the other room. (*To Kate*) Only for a few moments. I must speak to your husband.

Frances takes Kate to the inner room

Is this to be official?

Tom Yes.

Laura You realize when you have told me I may have to take . . .

Tom (*quietly*) Yes.

Laura Then I think Kate should be present to listen.

Tom If you say so.

Laura (*calling*) Miss Treadgold . . .

Frances comes into the doorway

Please bring back Kate.

Frances looks into the inner room, as if calling Kate

(*To Tom*) When you are ready.

Tom pauses a second, then rises and moves his chair down stage centre

Tom (*slowly*) The catharsis came—one evening—about eighteen months ago . . .

The Lights fade slowly to a Black-Out. A curtain drops, shutting off the main set

Tom exits into the wings, talking without a break

I came home elated. The Chairman had sent for me that afternoon. I couldn't believe my luck: and I couldn't wait to tell Kate. When I came in she was standing by the cot as usual—

The Lights come up to half. Kate is bending over a wicker cot, murmuring soothingly. She wears a long housecoat which completely covers her prison dress

—but this time, I didn't mind. I called—

Tom enters from the wings

—Kate—Kate—wonderful news.
Kate (*without turning*) Dinner's almost ready.
Tom Damn dinner. I want to talk to you.
Kate Ssh. I think she's asleep. There, there, my pretty.
Tom Pretty. Sweet Christ. (*He moves away and mimes pouring out drinks*)
Kate She's been so good today. Do you know, she actually seemed to know.
Tom Kate, will you come here. Now, drink this.

Kate moves towards Tom, but still looks back at the cot.

Kate, will you look at me. (*He turns her head and snaps his fingers*) Come back. I'm your husband, darling. Remember?
Kate Yes, Tom—of course.
Tom So drink that. Go on—drink it.

They mime drinking and Tom's taking back the glass

Now, listen to me for just five minutes. I've got that transfer.
Kate Trans . . . ?
Tom To manage the Toronto branch.
Kate Toronto . . . (*She obviously pulls herself together*) Oh, Tom, I'm so glad for you.
Tom For me? For us. Don't you realize? It's a new life.
Kate It's an uprooting.
Tom It's wonderful. Nearly double the salary. A free passage out there. And there's a house, Kate, with a garden, and a pool.
Kate A pool? A safe pool?
Tom (*laughing*) Well, what else?
Kate She'll like that. She might even swim. Tom, do you think she might learn to swim?

Tom Kate . . .

Kate I'm sure she's improving. This morning she stared at me—do you know—I really think she focused.

Tom Stop it, can't you!

Kate But . . .

Tom I come home—feeling ten feet tall—bursting with tremendous news. Can't you drag your thoughts away from—from that—even for a moment?

Kate (*coaxing*) Come and look at her. Please. Just one look.

Tom I don't want to look at it. It shouldn't be here.

Kate Don't say that.

Tom I should have been firm in the beginning. It should be in a home. With its own kind. And people properly trained to look after it.

Kate (*quietly*) It's our child. We have a responsibility.

Tom Responsibility to what? A set of paralysed muscles and a non-existent brain?

Kate Don't let's go over all that again. (*She goes and looks in the cot, then returns to him, changing her tone*) Tell me more about the job.

Tom (*abruptly*) Do you remember the christening?

Kate Tom—the job . . .

Tom I shall never forget it. That embarrassed little group round the font. Godparents making impossible promises . . .

Kate We agreed . . .

Tom Even the priest—he didn't say "receive and bless this child"—he said "receive and help this child. He should have said "God help the parents and the other children of this marriage". And it lay there in his arms—a mass of frills and lace—decked out like a bloody sacrifice.

Kate Tom!

Tom Only we were the sacrifice. And I won't be sacrificed any longer—seeing you devoted to a vegetable—a nothing.

Kate How can you think that?

Tom Do you think of me? Or the boys?

Kate The boys love her.

Tom Don't be blasphemous.

Kate They do.

Tom You think so? I'll tell you something. When David's puppy was run over—he said to me, "Why couldn't she have been destroyed instead?"

Kate Don't keep saying "she" and "it". If you remember the christening so well, you may also remember she had two good names!

Tom Only one is applicable. Monster!

Kate (*crying out in anguish*) Tom!

Tom (*now beside himself*) Yes, I've said it at last. Monster!

Kate strikes out at him across the face. They look at each other. Suddenly she collapses in the upright chair. He kneels down, putting his arms round her

Kate Oh God, I'm sorry—I'm sorry . . .

Tom (*gently*) Listen, love. I do understand. It's my child, too, you know. My seed. Do you suppose I've not felt humiliated? And guilty?

Kate No-one is guilty. It happens.

Tom Yes, and must be dealt with. This is it, Kate. This is the decision.

Kate Decision?

Tom Yes. I take this job. We go overseas, where we are not known. You and I and the boys.

Kate You mean . . . ?

Tom A normal family, Kate. Free. And forgetting.

Kate looks at him blankly, then draws away

Kate No, Tom.

Tom It'll take time. But we can adjust. We're still young. And intelligent —at least, I hope we are.

Kate I couldn't live with myself.

Tom (*moving away; quietly*) The question is—are you going to live with me?

Kate What do you mean?

Tom I want my wife, Kate. And the boys want their mother.

Kate I've never neglected you.

Tom Physically, no. Mentally, we don't exist.

Kate That's not fair!

Tom It's the ugly truth. No, Kate, I want "out". I'm sick of this—this bitterness and resentment. It wasn't too much to ask, was it? Another child—a normal girl child. A simple biological process. And we had to get . . .

Kate Don't say it again!

Tom Be sensible. That—it—won't always stay small and helpless. Do you realize? It's going to grow . . .

Kate We'll face that when the time comes.

Tom It's fifteen months old. It could be fifteen years—twenty-five. Adult. Do you think you can still cope? No. I've reached my limit. I want this job. I've worked for it.

Kate Then go without me.

Tom *Kate!*

Kate Be free. If that's what you want.

Tom Is that what *you* want?

Kate It is you who said that there must be a decision.

Tom And you could let me go? With the boys? Oh, have no doubts—I'd take the boys.

Kate (*not really listening*) There could be a breakthrough in research—in drugs. One day she might be normal.

Tom In the name of sanity, stop deluding yourself. All the experts have told us from the beginning. Look the facts in the face. (*Deliberately*) There is no hope.

Kate There is patience. We must wait.

Tom And what happens while we're waiting? You're already worn out— at twenty-eight. What's left for me? When I touch you—what happens? You're under stress—exhausted. Don't you understand? Must I say it again? I want my wife. (*He pulls her roughly into his arms*)

Kate resists, falling on her knees

Kate No—Tom—no . . .
Tom Kate . . .
Kate I can't . . .
Tom (*suddenly losing control*) By God, you can, and you shall.
Kate (*fighting him off*) Leave me alone . . .

A child's voice calls off, followed by banging

That's David.
Tom So what?
Kate He'll keep banging.
Tom Let him.
Kate He'll wake her. (*She breaks away, runs to the cot and looks in*)

Kate exits, calling

(*As she goes*) I'm coming. I'm coming. Stop that noise.

Tom stands shivering and shaking. He loosens his collar and wipes his forehead. He does a mime pouring a drink as before, and lifting it. Then he mimes throwing it down. The glass is heard smashing. He speaks very low

Tom God Almighty . . . (*He turns to look at the cot, then goes slowly and stands by it, his head bent. Then he forces himself to look. He goes rigid. Then he pulls out the pillow and presses it down in the cot. He holds it there for a moment, then raises it and looks down. He makes a faint retching sound, and throws down the pillow. He stands looking into the cot*)

Kate enters and steps on the broken glass. It is heard to crunch

Kate You've broken a glass. (*She sees him by the cot and her face lights up. She goes to him*) Oh, Tom. You've looked at her. At last. Dear Tom. (*She looks into the cot. Her voice trails off*) Dear—Tom . . .

He swings away by the chair. She looks after him. Then she makes swift movements as if examining the dead child. After a second, she pulls up the sheet and tucks it in neatly. She picks up the pillow. Then she wheels the cot away

Kate exits with the cot

Tom stands stiffly by the chair, then collapses into it, his head in his hands

Kate returns, walking like an automaton. She carries a brush and pan

Kate (*blankly*) I must sweep up this glass.

They look at each other across the room. Tom sobs harshly once. Kate drops the pan and brush, goes and puts her arms round him protectively

(*Quietly*) S—hush. It's all right.

Tom Sheila's dead. (*Puzzled*) Sheila. That's funny. I can say her name.
Quite suddenly—I can say her name.

Kate (*abruptly*) I've prayed for this.

Tom What?

Kate You don't know how often, when I've been alone here, I've prayed
for it. And now it's happened. (*Very quietly*) Thank God.

Tom You're in shock. You don't realize. I've killed the child.

Kate No. I have.

Tom Kate . . .

Kate If I had been sensible and let her go away, she'd still be alive. It's
my fault.

Tom No.

Kate I realized how wrong I'd been when I—looked at her just now.
(*Quietly*) There was—no more life, you see. It makes it all so different.

Tom (*getting up*) We'll get the doctor. (*He goes and mimes picking up the
telephone*)

Kate (*sitting*) It won't be any use.

Tom You need help. (*He mimes dialling, which is heard*)

Kate And he'll have to tell the police.

Tom stops in the act of dialling

Tom The police. (*He mimes putting down the telephone. It all suddenly
becomes too much*) Kate, what are we going to do?

Kate Tell him I did it.

Tom (*aghast*) You what . . . ? Are you out of your mind?

Kate No. I can think again now. It's perfectly clear in my mind. We have
to protect the boys.

Tom Yes, but . . .

Kate If you go to prison, you'll lose your job.

Tom It may not come to that.

Kate We can't take the risk.

Tom We'll see. (*He turns as if to phone again*)

Kate (*grabbing his arm*) Listen to me! You must listen to me!

Tom (*putting his arms round her; quietly*) All right, love. All right. But it
won't make any difference. I . . .

Kate Are you listening?

Tom Yes.

Kate (*moving away with her back to him*) If they knew I did it, they are
sure to be sympathetic. I may get off lightly, but if you go to prison your
job will be finished. I shall have to wait on alone. And afterwards, you'll
have to start again, with a record.

Tom You are not taking the blame.

Kate You said you would listen.

Tom But . . .

Kate I've not finished.

Tom makes a hopeless gesture

The company have been good to you. I know they would help if you
asked them to wait and send you abroad when this is over. Then we
could really start again.

Tom No, Kate.

Kate That's what you wanted—to start again—free.

Tom Not on such terms.

Kate (*feverishly*) I know I'm right. It's my fault. And I should pay for it.

Tom (*bitterly*) We shall all have to pay for it.

Kate Not my way. No, my mind is made up. I shall say I did it and go on
saying so. If you argue, you'll only confuse things. Then they may
punish us both.

Tom If they do . . .

Kate (*abruptly*) What will happen to the boys?

Tom begins to waver

Tom (*quietly*) Oh, my God!

Kate This is the right way.

Tom I can't do it.

Kate (*going to him*) Yes, you can. You must. It'll work. You'll see. (*She
pauses, putting her hand to her head. Slowly*) I must clear that glass. (*She
goes on her knees and starts to sweep*)

*He kneels beside her, putting a hand over hers. She sits back on her heels.
They look at each other*

Tom Kate, love . . .

Kate (*suddenly*) Oh, Tom—my baby. My poor, poor baby . . . (*She breaks
down in his arms*)

*The Lights fade slowly to a Black-Out, then return slowly to full. Laura is
at her desk, Tom standing before it, his hand on the back of a chair, his head
bent. Kate sits on the window-seat with Frances above her*

Tom So that's it, madam. Now you know.

Laura Thank you for telling me.

Tom (*abruptly*) How soon can Kate be released?

Laura I couldn't possibly tell you that.

Tom She's been here for something she didn't do—and she's been beaten
for it . . .

Laura Mr Walmer . . .

Tom I want to make a written statement.

Laura Before you say anything more, I must tell you Kate wasn't attacked
because she had—supposedly—killed her child.

Tom (*blankly*) Not . . . ?

Kate Why did you have to be so headlong?

Laura I thought you'd been told. (*She looks at Frances*)

Frances He was too distraught to listen.

Tom I am not distraught now.

Laura Kate will explain to you. The offenders have been punished.

Tom It makes no difference. May I make the statement now?

Laura If you wish.

Tom I do.

Laura (*gently*) I want you to think carefully. Once you have made this statement and signed it—the matter is official. Will you please be very sure that is what you want?

Kate looks up hopefully

Tom I am sure.

Kate Please . . .

Laura Will you go with Kate and talk it over first?

Tom No. She is stronger than I am. She might persuade me. I let her persuade me before, and it was wrong.

Kate But . . .

Tom No, Kate. (*Going urgently to the desk*) Madam, help me.

Laura (*quietly*) Very well.

Kate sobs once more. Frances puts an arm round her

Please sit down.

Tom sits at the desk. Laura gives him the paper and pen

Before you sign, let me see it.

Tom Yes, madam. (*He starts writing*)

Laura flicks the intercom

Laura This is the Governor speaking. Please ask the Chief Officer to come to my office. Thank you.

Laura waits while Tom finishes. He passes her the sheet. She reads it

(*Quietly*) That is very concise. Now I want you to add a paragraph which I will dictate. (*She passes the paper back*)

Tom writes as she dictates

I have made this statement voluntarily—at my own request. I have not been influenced . . .

There is a knock at the door

(*Calling*) One moment, please. Not been influenced—in any manner whatsoever in the making of it.

Laura waits. He looks up

Have you got that?

Tom Yes.

Laura (*gently*) Now you may sign.

Tom signs. Laura watches as he does so

Please add the date after your signature.

Tom finishes writing, stands up, and looks at the paper in his hand. Kate

*gets up abruptly. Tom looks over to her. For a second there is tense silence
between them. Then Tom puts the paper on the desk and moves sharply away,
his back half towards the audience. Kate sobs. Frances puts a hand on her
arm*

Thank you. (*Calling*) Come in.

Probyn enters

Chief, please have Kate taken back to the hospital.
Tom (*turning*) But . . .
Laura Mr Walmer is to go with her. They may have two hours together.
I shall want to see them again before he leaves.
Probyn Yes, madam.

Probyn opens the main door and stands waiting

Collins is seen outside

Laura Please ask Sister to let them have the small sitting-room so that
they can talk privately.
Tom But I must know what happens next.
Kate Tom—please—(*she runs to him*)—we must leave this to the Governor.
Tom I can't . . .
Kate (*urgently*) Tom, please. Not now. (*She puts her arm through his and
turns to Laura*) I did not want this to happen. I'm sorry. We—we will
do whatever you say. (*She takes Tom to the door, and turns*) I know you
will be fair.

Kate and Tom exit through the main door. Probyn follows

Frances What a mess. What a pathetic, damnable mess.
Laura Yes. (*She looks at Tom's statement, then puts it aside and picks up
the telephone*) This is the Governor speaking. Will you get me the Home
Office—Prisons Department.
Frances Laura . . .

Laura gestures for silence

Laura I wish to speak to the Chief Director, Women's Prisons. If he is not
available I will speak to the Assistant Director . . . Thank you. (*She
replaces the receiver*)
Frances Laura—you're not going to refer this?
Laura What else?
Frances There can only be one answer. The matter will be passed to the
police.
Laura (*quietly*) Yes.
Frances I don't have to tell you the sequence. He will be charged,
remanded—and committed for trial. All that agony to live through
again—what they have done will have been for nothing . . .

Laura (*breaking in*) We will hope not.

Frances Laura, let it alone. It need go no further. Kate has only a few weeks left . . .

Laura You cannot think I have any choice.

Frances Of course you have a choice.

Laura (*picking up the paper*) With this in my hand?

Frances He should not have been encouraged to make it.

Laura That is incorrect. You heard me do everything possible to avoid it.

Frances You should not have let him tell you in the first place.

Laura Could you have foreseen what he was going to say?

Frances It is still only between the four of us. I shall repeat nothing. And think back—to that remark of Kate's. "We shall do whatever you say."

Laura He wanted to make this statement. For eighteen months he has lived a lie.

Frances He could still be swayed.

Laura Are you asking me to stand between a man and his conscience?

Frances Damn conscience! This is a matter of survival—(*working up*)—the survival of a whole family . . .

Frances stops

Laura Frances (*quietly*) You must not be emotional.

Frances I would not be human if I were not emotional at this moment.

Laura That is understandable. But you must use your self-control.

Frances How can you say that! Are you made of stone?

Laura (*half to herself*) It might be easier if I were.

Frances Then let me appeal to you. Don't do it, Laura. Don't start this wretched business again. He would lose his job. And how will he get another, with such a charge? They will be destitute.

Laura You are running ahead of yourself. Juries are not made of stone either.

Frances We can't risk that.

Laura We?

Frances You, then. If you must sit in judgement, at least let it be merciful.

Laura We are not here to judge. It is not our province.

Frances You're a hard woman.

Laura If that's your judgement, you're entitled to think so.

The telephone rings. Laura picks up the receiver

Frances Laura—please . . .

Laura Hullo? . . . Yes, I see. Connect me as soon as possible. (*She replaces the receiver*) There is a delay in getting through to London. (*She starts sorting papers on the desk*)

Frances (*urgently*) Then we've still a chance. Laura, cancel that call.

Laura What!

Frances Cancel that call.

Laura (*quietly*) Don't be foolish. (*She returns to her papers*)

Frances Is there nothing I can do . . .

Laura I think it would be better if you went away and left me to deal with this. After all, it's entirely my decision.

Frances How does that help the issue?

Laura It may relieve your conscience and make it easier for both of us.

Frances I don't want to make it easier for you. I want you to realize what you are doing.

Laura (*suddenly*) Do you think I don't? Do you think I want to do this?

Frances Then tear up that paper.

Laura Tear . . . Are you out of your mind?

Frances Give it to me and see.

Laura You would—deliberately—conceal the truth?

Frances Truth? What is the truth?

Laura swings round, half facing the audience. She takes off her spectacles and passes her hand over her eyes. She looks very tired

Laura Someone asked that—two thousand years ago. I can't remember it helped him to make the right decision either.

Frances Then you do doubt it is the right decision.

Laura I am not empowered to make any decision in these circumstances.

Frances If you refer it, you will ruin their lives.

Laura That is not a foregone conclusion.

Frances But you admit the risk. Oh, I know what I would do if I were in your position.

Laura Be thankful you are not. Please go, Frances. (*She returns to her papers*)

Frances (*slowly*) I had a chance to be.

Laura (*glancing up*) To be . . . ?

Frances In your position.

Laura That is in the future. (*She begins to write*)

Frances Not with your approval. And you would not speak for me now.

Laura (*quietly*) This is irrelevant.

Frances It is not. You have never been in favour of my being governor.

Laura I have not said so.

Frances You did not need to.

Laura Please—you know we cannot discuss this.

Frances I . . .

Laura Frances. (*She throws down her pen, rises, and goes to Frances. Gently*) I know how you feel—oh yes, I do. Believe me, I do. But you are seeing this out of all proportion.

Frances How else can I see it?

Laura As a simple matter of prison procedure. You and I have discussed it and you have—perfectly correctly—expressed your views. If I do not agree with them, it is not your responsibility.

Frances It is my responsibility to try and persuade you.

Laura I can only do what I know I have to do. One day you may well find yourself in the same position.

Frances No, I shall not. Because if you do this, I shall resign.

Laura (*half exasperated*) Oh, don't be ridiculous.

Frances (*slowly*) I once said—it had been a privilege to work with you. After this, I could not work with you at all. (*She faces Laura straightly*) I mean that.

Laura Frances, you are being dramatic. Go away and calm down. Otherwise you may well do something you will regret.

Frances What can it matter to you? In a few weeks, you will retire. Would it be so terrible—just for once—to bend the rules? You have the discretion to act . . .

Laura (*beginning to show signs of strain*) Once and for all—will you stop . . .

Frances (*relentlessly*) Or are you looking ahead? To the Honours List?

There is a grim pause. Laura steps back

Laura (*very low*) How dare you even think . . .

Frances You are afraid to show compassion and be found out. You are prepared to sacrifice two people for the sake of a possible O.B.E.

Laura (*in a whisper*) That is an—infamous suggestion. (*Shaken, she turns to the desk, her back to Frances*)

Frances You are going to do an infamous thing. And if this is part of the job, I want nothing of it.

Laura Please—leave my office.

Frances goes to the main door, then turns, speaking across to Laura's rigid back

Frances (*quietly*) I—should not have said that. I know it can't be unsaid, but I'm sorry. Believe me, Laura, I am—truly sorry.

Laura (*very low*) Thank you.

Frances You are right, of course.

Laura Right?

Frances I should not make a good governor. I am too impulsive. It is not enough to do the wrong thing for the right reasons. I do not have your strength. Perhaps later, out of that strength—you will find you can—forgive me. (*She opens the door*)

Laura (*turning*) Frances . . .

The intercom buzzes. Laura flicks it

Yes?

A voice is heard through the intercom

Voice Madam, your call is coming through from the Home Office. The Chief Director is on the line.

Laura Thank you. Put him through.

Frances (*gently*) You can still do it. You need only refer the matter of Valentine and Gow. Oh, Laura—think. Please—think.

Frances goes out, shutting the door

Laura takes the statement from the desk and moves away, reading it. The

*telephone starts to ring. She looks across at it. She does not move. The
telephone continues to ring insistently. She goes to the desk and picks it up.
She waits a second longer before actually putting it to her ear.*

Laura (*steadily*) This is the Governor speaking . . .

CURTAIN

FURNITURE AND PROPERTY LIST

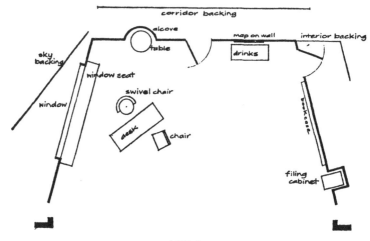

ACT I

On stage: Desk. *On it:* telephone, intercom, folders with papers, silver cigarette box with cigarettes, ashtray, matches, pen tray with pens, pencils, elastic bands, letter tray with papers, blotter. *In drawer:* bunch of keys, ruler
Swivel chair
Small chair
Drinks table. *On it:* 6 glasses, brandy, whisky, soda syphon
Alcove table
Filing cabinet. *In it:* files
Bookshelves. *In them:* books, 1 folded newspaper
Window-seat
Window curtains
Carpet
On wall: prison plan

Off stage: Clipboard of papers (Frances)
Bouquet of flowers in cellophane with letter in envelope (Marcy)
Basket of papers, letters and a photograph (Marian)
Tray with 2 cups and saucers, spoons, coffee-pot, milk jug, sugar bowl (Marcy)
Torch (Dr Graham)
Carafe of water and glass (Collins)
Bottles of tablets (Dr Graham)

Coffee-pot (**Collins**)
Overcoat for Kate (**Collins**)
Yellow duster with four cigarettes folded inside (**Marcy**)
Notebook and pencil (**Marian**)
Report book (**Probyn**)
Suitcase (**Probyn**)

Personal: **Laura:** handbag with spectacles
Dr Graham: spectacles
Laura: watch
Rev. John: small notebook with pencil

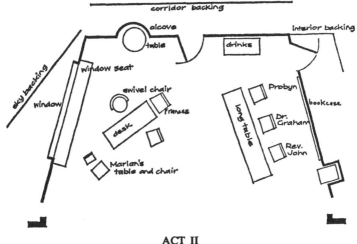

ACT II

Scene 1

Strike: Everything on desk except telephone, intercom, 4 folders, pentray

Set: Long narrow table across stage from desk. *On it:* silver cigarette box
(full), ashtray, matches
3 small chairs behind long table
Small square table below desk. *On it:* 5 notebooks, 5 pencils. (This
table may be omitted if space is limited, and the props set on the
desk.)
Small chair behind table
On alcove table: copy of *The Times*

Off stage: Table napkin (**Laura**)
Tray of used lunch dishes (**Marcy**)
Note on two pieces of toilet paper (**Marcy**)
Yellow duster with watch in special pocket (**Mary**)
Notebook and pencil (**Marian**)

Envelope containing photographs (**Dr Graham**)
Papers (**Probyn**)
Flat piece of wood wrapped in sacking or canvas (**Probyn**)

Personal: **Rev. John**: watch on chain, book

SCENE 2

Set: *On desk:* letter tray and blotter, Marian's notebook and pencil, Valentine's folder

Off stage: Tray of used tea-things (**Marcy**)

Personal: **Rev. John**: handkerchief

ACT III

Strike: Chair below desk

Set: Ruler in desk drawer
Piece of wood on floor by desk

Off stage: Kidney dish with cotton-wool and syringe (**Probyn**)
Long housecoat (**Kate**)
Baby's cot, with wrapped doll, cover and pillow (**Kate**)
Brush and pan (**Kate**)

Special note: The Watch Trick. Two watches are needed. One on its chain in the Chaplain's pocket, the other without chain in a special pocket made in the yellow duster. When Marcy dusts the Chaplain's watch she can slip it off the chain, tuck the watch and chain back in his pocket and pat the pocket. This leaves the loose chain ready for him to produce, and the other watch ready in the duster.

LIGHTING PLOT

Property fittings required: nil

Interior. An office. The same scene throughout

ACT I. Morning

To open: General effect of morning light

No cues

ACT II, SCENE 1. Afternoon

To open: General effect of afternoon light

No cues

ACT II, SCENE 2. Afternoon

To open: As previous scene

No cues

ACT III. Afternoon

To open: As previous scene

Cue 1	**Tom:** ". . . about eighteen months ago"	(Page 60)
	Fade to Black-Out, then bring up spots on downstage area	
Cue 2	**Kate:** "My poor, poor baby"	(Page 65)
	Fade to Black-Out, then bring up to previous full area lighting	

EFFECTS PLOT

ACT I

ACT II

SCENE 1

SCENE 2

ACT III

Lightning Source UK Ltd.
Milton Keynes UK
UKOW06f0719260915

259315UK00001B/20/P